The Workbook on Spiritual Disciplines

The Workbook on Spiritual Disciplines

Maxie D. Dunnam

The Upper Room

Nashville, Tennessee

The Workbook on Spiritual Disciplines

Photo credits (in order of appearance): John Netherton; Religious News Service; Don Johnson; Religious News Service; Julie Clifford; John Netherton

Scripture quotations not otherwise identified are from the Revised Standard Version of the Bible, copyrighted 1946, 1952, and © 1971 by the Division of Christian Education, National Council of the Churches of Christ in the United States of America, and are used by permission.

Scripture quotations designated JB are from *The Jerusalem Bible,* copyright © 1966 by Darton, Longman & Todd, Ltd. and Doubleday and Company, Inc. Used by permission of the publisher.

Scripture quotations designated NEB are from *The New English Bible,* © The Delegates of the Oxford University Press and the Syndics of the Cambridge University Press 1961 and 1970, and are reprinted by permission.

Scripture quotations designated Phillips are from the *The New Testament in Modern English* by J. B. Phillips. Copyright © 1958, by J. B. Phillips. Reprinted with permission of the Macmillan Company.

Scripture quotations designated NKJV are from *The New King James Version.* Copyright © 1979, 1980, 1982, Thomas Nelson, Inc., Publishers.

Scripture quotations designated KJV are from the King James Version of the Bible.

Scripture quotations designated AP are the author's paraphrase.

Selected lines from *A Hundred Years' War: The Salvation Army 1865-1965* by Bernard Watson, published by Hodder & Stoughton, are used by permission of Salvationist Publishing and Supplies Ltd. (London).

Selected lines from "Ash-Wednesday" in COLLECTED POEMS 1909-1962 by T.S. Eliot, copyright 1936 by Harcourt Brace Jovanovich, Inc.; copyright © 1963, 1964 by T.S. Eliot, are used by permission of Harcourt Brace Jovanovich, Inc. and Faber and Faber Publishers (London).

Excerpts from CLOWNING IN ROME by Henri J.M. Nouwen, copyright © 1979 by Henri J.M. Nouwen, are reprinted by permission of Doubleday & Company.

Excerpts from TOGETHER IN SOLITUDE by Douglas V. Steere, copyright © 1982 by Douglas V. Steere, are used by permission of The Crossroad Publishing Company.

Excerpts from LOVE AND WILL by Rollo May, copyright © 1969 by W.W. Norton & Company, Inc., are used by permission of W.W. Norton and Souvenir Press Ltd. (London).

Excerpts from *When God Was Man* by J.B. Phillips, copyright 1955 by Abingdon Press, are used by permission of the publisher.

Selected lines from *Tell Me Again, Lord, I Forget* by Ruth Harms Calkin, published by David C. Cook Publishing Co., are used by permission of the author.

Book Design: Harriette Bateman
First Printing: June, 1984 (15)
Second Printing: September, 1984 (20)
Third Printing: March, 1986 (15)
Fourth Printing: March, 1987 (15)
Fifth Printing: March, 1988 (25)
Sixth Printing: September, 1991 (10)
Seventh Printing: April, 1993 (20)
ISBN 0-8358-0479-8

Printed in the United States of America

Contents

6. Generosity

Introduction

During the Los Angeles Open Golf Tournament a few years ago, Arnold Palmer, the legendary golfer, was interviewed while practicing on the putting green. "Arnie, what do you feel was wrong to make you play so poorly this past year?" he was asked.

Without looking up from his putting, Arnold answered in his own direct way, "I wasn't hard enough on myself, that's all."

Two hours after this brief interview, the same reporter came back to find Palmer still practicing on the putting green. The reporter concluded, "The greatness of Arnold Palmer is his choice of the hard way."

Without knowing it, Arnold Palmer brought some understanding to one of the seemingly severe demands of Jesus.

> Enter by the narrow gate; for the gate is wide and the way is easy, that leads to destruction, and those who enter by it are many. For the gate is narrow and the way is hard, that leads to life, and those who find it are few.
>
> —Matthew 7:13–14

There is no mistaking meaning here. Jesus' command is as clear as it is challenging. There is in life a broad and easy way. Most of us take that way most of the time. The end is destruction. There is a narrow and hard way. Some, too few, take that way. Following the narrow, hard way leads to life. The difference between these two ways is that of the undisciplined life and the disciplined life.

There is an old adage which claims that practice makes perfect. It rolls off our tongues so easily, yet if we really hear, it lays a great claim upon us. Like all generalities, it is not completely true but it has more than enough truth in it to make it an authentic call upon our lives.

We know, for example, the arduous practice to which a master

7

musician must be committed. As we listen to a great pianist, we know that the superb performance did not come without the toil and sweat of repetitious labor—without discipline. But it is also true in efforts other than music.

Plato's *Republic* begins with a very simple sentence: "I went down yesterday to the Piraeus with Glaucon the son of Ariston, that I might offer up my prayers to the goddess...." According to the original manuscript in his own handwriting, Plato had thirteen different versions of that opening sentence. This paragon *practiced* his art, labored tirelessly to get the sentence just right. No wonder *The Republic* is a peerless example of the writing art.

What we know to be true in athletics and the arts is also true in our Christian life. We grow by disciplined effort, by intentional design, by decision and will. This workbook is designed to assist you in your program of spiritual growth.

Discipline is an absolute necessity for the Christian life. We may be converted to Christ in the miracle of a moment, but becoming a saint is the task of a lifetime. And we are called to sainthood. We are to *grow up* in Christ (Eph. 4:15), to become mature in Christ (Col. 1:28), and to have the mind of Christ in us (Phil. 2:5). Paul used the metaphor of childbirth to express his groaning desire that Christians grow to the measure of the stature of the fullness of Christ. "Oh, my dear children, I feel the pangs of childbirth all over again till Christ be formed within you" (Gal. 4:19, Phillips).

As Christians we do not emerge full-blown; we grow. We grow by discipline. So let's be clear as we begin. Discipline is not an end in itself. In the history of Christianity that thought has not always prevailed, and disciplines themselves have become *the thing*. We have made discipline an end, not a means. We have even used it as a proof of our "sainthood." That is the reason Christianity is often presented as a somber, self-denying, world-denying way that produces pinch-faced sadness. Jesus presented something else. He called us to the joy of a wedding banquet, to the dance of celebration over a lost son who has come home. But we experience that freedom of joy and celebration only as we are willing to see the kingdom as a pearl of great price for which we are willing to exchange all else.

The best contemporary book on this theme I know is Richard J. Foster's *Celebration of Discipline*. I had intended to write this workbook in 1980, but Foster's book was published in 1978 and I felt it was, in a marked way, the only word needed. With the prodding of the editors of The Upper Room I finally decided that this workbook format would make a positive contribution to persons' being able to *work at* a disciplined life. Foster's title communicates a truth. *Celebration* and *discipline* go together. The purpose of discipline is to liberate us—to free us from, rather than sentence us to, bondage. Discipline enables us to exchange lesser values, habits, styles, attitudes, ways of relating, limited understandings, closed minds, for the pearl of great price, the kingdom. So rather than misery, discipline is to bring joy. Richard Foster says it well:

> Neither should we think of the Spiritual Disciplines as some dull drudgery aimed at exterminating laughter from the face of the earth. Joy is the keynote of all the Disciplines. The purpose of the Disciplines is liberation from the stifling slavery to self-interest and fear. When one's inner spirit is set free from all that holds it down, that can hardly be described as dull drudgery. Singing, dancing, even shouting characterize the Disciplines of the spiritual life. (Foster, p. 2).

At an earlier time (1947) Albert Day wrote a manual for The Disciplined Order of Christ entitled *Discipline and Discovery.* Along with *Celebration of Discipline,* it is a contemporary classic on spiritual discipline. I recommend both of these books. Albert Edward Day very helpfully cautions us with three clear words. One, discipline must not be practiced for its own sake. Two, discipline must not be confused with repression. Three, discipline must never be conceived as a denial or destruction of your own uniqueness.

The purpose of this workbook is to help the reader grow spiritually. As indicated earlier, the Christian is to grow up *in Christ.* So the goal of our life is to be formed in Christ, to take the Christ-shape for our own being.

There is no way, in the scope of such an effort, to deal with all the disciplines necessary for spiritual growth. Each reader will wonder why I did not address a particular discipline. Two of the most obvious ones left out are worship and fasting, both classic spiritual disciplines. Limited by space, I made a decision not to include these. Worship is probably the most commonly practiced Christian discipline, therefore it does get a lot of attention otherwise. Fasting is a discipline that demands more attention than the limited focus I could have given it in this workbook.

Also, as is always the case with me, I write out of my own *need,* as well as my own experience, and this was the way it came out. My prayer is that what is here will be only the beginning of each reader's pursuit of a disciplined life of spiritual growth. There is no pretension about providing anything final. I am only, as Daniel Niles said in *That They May Have Life,* one beggar telling another beggar where to find bread.

THE PLAN

Here is the plan. This is a six-week adventure. It is an individual journey, but my hope is that you will share it with some fellow pilgrims who will meet together once each week during the six weeks of the study. You are asked to give thirty minutes each day to learn about and appropriate the disciplines for spiritual growth. For most persons these thirty minutes will come at the beginning of the day. However, if it is not possible for you to give the time at the beginning of the day, do it whenever the time is available—but do it regularly. The purpose of this spiritual journey must not be forgotten: to incorporate these disciplines into your daily life.

The workbook is arranged in six major divisions, each designed to guide you for one week. These divisions contain seven sections, one for each day of the week. Each day of the week will have two major aspects: reading about the discipline, and reflecting and recording.

Reading about the Discipline

In each day's section you will read something about discipline— not too much, but enough to provide something of the nature, meaning, and possibilities of growth through discipline. Included in this will be some portions of scripture. The scripture is a basic resource for Christian discipline and living. Quotations from sources other than scripture are followed by the author's name and the page number on which the quote can be found. These citations are keyed to the "References" section at the back of the workbook where you will find complete bibliographic information for each source.

Reflecting and Recording

Then each day, there will be a time for reflecting and recording. This dimension calls you to record some of your reflections. The degree of meaning you receive from this workbook is largely dependent upon your faithfulness to its practice. You may be unable on a particular day to do precisely what is requested. If so, then simply record that fact and make a note of why you can't follow through. This may give you insight about yourself and help you to grow.

Also, on some days there may be more suggestions than you can deal with in the time you have. Do what is most meaningful for you, and don't feel *guilty*.

The emphasis is upon growth, not perfection. Don't feel guilty if you do not follow exactly the pattern of the days. Follow the content and direction seriously, but not slavishly. Always remember that this is a personal pilgrimage. What you write in your personal workbook is your private property. You may not wish to share it with anyone. For this reason, no two people should attempt to share the same workbook. The importance of what you write is not what it may mean to someone else, but what it means to you. Writing, even if it is only brief notes or single-word reminders, helps us clarify our feelings and thinking.

The significance of the reflecting and recording dimensions will grow as you move along. Even beyond the six-week period, you will find meaning in looking back to what you wrote on a particular day in response to a particular situation.

SHARING WITH OTHERS

In the history of Christian piety, the spiritual director or guide has been a significant person. To varying degrees most of us have had spiritual directors—persons to whom we have turned for support and direction in our spiritual pilgrimage. There is a sense in which this workbook can be a spiritual guide, for you can use it as a private venture without participating in a group.

Its meaning will be enhanced, however, if you share the adventure with eight to twelve others. In this way, the "priesthood of all believers" will come alive, and you will profit from the growing insights of others, and they will profit from yours. A guide for group sharing is included in the text at the end of each week.

If this is a group venture, all persons should begin their personal involvement with the workbook on the same day, so that when you come together to share as a group all will have been dealing with the same material and will be at the same place in the text. It will be helpful if you have an initial get-acquainted group meeting to begin the adventure. A guide for this meeting is provided in this introduction.

Group sessions for this workbook are designed to last one and one-half hours (with the exception of this initial meeting). Those sharing in the group should covenant to attend all sessions unless an emergency prevents attendance. There will be six weekly sessions following this first get-acquainted time.

A group consisting of eight to twelve members is about the right size. Larger numbers limit individual involvement.

One person can provide the leadership for the entire six weeks, or leaders can be assigned from week to week. The leader's task:
- to read directions and determine ahead of time how to handle the session. It may not be possible to use all the suggestions for sharing and praying together. Feel free to select those you think will be most meaningful and those for which you have adequate time.
- to model a style of openness, honesty, and warmth. A leader

should not ask others to share what he or she is not willing to share. Usually the leader should be the first to share, especially as it relates to personal experiences.
- to moderate the discussion.
- to encourage reluctant members to participate, and try to prevent a few persons from doing all the talking.
- to keep the sharing centered in personal experience, rather than academic debate.
- to honor the time schedule. If it appears necessary to go longer than one and one-half hours, the leader should get consensus for continuing another twenty or thirty minutes.
- to see that meeting time and place are known by all, especially if meetings are held in different homes.
- to make sure necessary materials for meetings are available and that the meeting room is arranged ahead of time.

It is desirable that weekly meetings be held in the homes of the participants. (Hosts or hostesses should make sure there are as few interruptions as possible, e.g., children, telephone, pets, etc.) If meetings are held in a church, they should be in an informal setting. Participants are asked to dress casually, to be comfortable and relaxed.

If refreshments are served, they should come after the meeting. In this way, those who wish to stay longer for informal discussion may do so, while those who need to keep to a specific time schedule will be free to leave, but will get the full value of the meeting time.

SUGGESTIONS FOR INITIAL GET-ACQUAINTED MEETING

Since the initial meeting is for the purpose of getting acquainted and beginning the shared pilgrimage, here is a way to get started. (If name tags are needed, provide them.)

1. Have each person in the group give his or her full name and the name by which each wishes to be called. Do away with titles. Address all persons by their first name or nickname. (Each person should make a list of the names somewhere in his/her workbook.)

2. Let each person in the group share one of the happiest, most exciting, or most meaningful experiences he/she has had during the past three or four weeks. After all persons have shared in this way, let the entire group sing the doxology ("Praise God, from Whom All Blessings Flow") or a chorus of praise.

3. After this experience of happy sharing, ask each person who will to share his/her expectations of the pilgrimage. Why did he or she become a part of it? What does each expect to gain from it? What are the reservations?

4. The leader should now review the introduction to the workbook and ask if there are questions about directions and procedures (this means that the leader should have read the introduction prior to the meeting). If persons have not received copies of the workbook, the books should be handed out now. *Remember that every person must have his/her own workbook.*

5. Day One in the workbook is the day following this initial meeting, and the next meeting should be held on Day Seven of the First Week. If the group must choose another weekly meeting time other than seven days from this initial session, the reading assignment should be brought in harmony with that so that the weekly meetings are always on Day Seven, and Day One is always the day following a weekly meeting.

6. Nothing binds a group together more than praying for one another. The leader should encourage each participant to write the names of each person in the group in his/her workbook, and commit to praying for them by name daily during this six weeks.

7. After checking to see that everyone knows the time and place of the next meeting, the leader may close with a prayer, thanking God for each person in the group, for the opportunity of growth, and for the possibility of growing through spiritual disciplines.

Special Note for Personal Schedule

Week Five is an emphasis on solitude and silence. It will be very meaningful if you can schedule a special time of silence—at least three hours, preferably an all-day silent retreat either during that week or immediately thereafter. Another possibility would be for the group to plan a twenty-four-hour retreat to experience *directed corporate silence*. The group should talk about this early and make whatever plans are necessary. A minister in your community or someone you know who has had retreat experience will be willing to help you with these plans. *A Journey Toward Solitude and Community* by Rueben Job is an excellent retreat resource.

Study, Scripture, and Guidance

Day One: *To Be a Disciple*

A disciple is one who subscribes to the teachings of a master and assists in spreading them. Any active adherent of a movment may be called a disciple.

Discipline is variously defined as training intended to produce a specified character or pattern of behavior, or the controlled behavior resulting from such training. From another perspective, discipline may be seen as punishment intended to correct or train, or it may be a set of rules or methods. We often refer to a branch of knowledge or teaching as a discipline. We talk about the different disciplines of an academic community, i.e., biology, philosophy, physics, history, sociology, etc.

In the context of the Christian faith, a disciple is not only one who subscribes to the teachings of Jesus and seeks to spread them, but one who seeks to relive Jesus' life in the world. Discipline for the Christian is the way we train ourselves or allow the Spirit to train us to be "like Jesus," to appropriate his spirit, and to cultivate the power to live his life in the world.

So discipleship means discipline. We have to work at being Christian. Since you are using this workbook, you already know that—at least you are pursuing some interest in the matter. The purpose of discipline for Christians is spiritual growth and ultimately our total transformation. Paul sounds our marching cadence:

> I appeal to you therefore, brethren, by the mercies of God, to present your bodies as a living sacrifice, holy and acceptable to God, which is your spiritual worship. Do not be conformed to this world but be transformed by the renewal of your mind, that you may prove what is the will of God, what is good and acceptable and perfect.
>
> —Romans 12:1–2

We are transformed by the renewal of our minds. We are what we think. So study is a necessary discipline for spiritual growth.

We must confess, shamefully, that study is not often high on the priority list of most Christians. In fact, there is a suspicion of learning in some churches and among many Christians. For some, to be "smart" and to be Christian are incongruent. There is a story out of the life of John Wesley that chides us here.

Wesley received a letter once from a pious brother who declared, "The Lord has directed me to write you that while you know Greek and Hebrew, he can do without your learning." Mr. Wesley replied appropriately, "Your letter received, and I may say in reply that your letter was superfluous as I already know that the Lord could do without my learning. I wish to say to you that while the Lord does not direct me to tell you, yet I feel impelled to tell you on my own responsibility, that the Lord does not need your ignorance either."

Jesus made it clear that knowledge is essential, absolutely essential: *knowledge of the truth.* "You will know the truth, and the truth will make you free" (John 8:32).

To Jesus' word we add Paul's word to Timothy, "Study to show thyself approved unto God, a workman that needeth not to be ashamed, rightly dividing the word of truth" (2 Tim. 2:15, KJV).

Paul is specifically addressing Timothy in his vocation, urging him to distinguish himself from the false teachers by being a teacher of the truth. Yet his word has general application to us. The phrase that is relevant to our discipline of study is "rightly dividing the word of truth." William Barclay provides unusual insight into this phrase by examining the Greek word for *rightly divide.*

> It is the word *orthotomein,* which literally means *to cut rightly.* It has many pictures in it. Calvin connected it with a father dividing out the food at a meal, and cutting it up so that each member of the family received the right and necessary and fitting portion. Beza connected it with the cutting up of sacrificial victims so that each part of the victim was correctly apportioned to the altar or to the priest. The Greeks themselves used the word, or the phrase, in three different connections. They used it for driving a straight road across country; they used it for ploughing a straight furrow across a field; they used it for the work of a mason in cutting and

squaring a stone so that it fitted into its correct place in the structure of the building. So the man who rightly divides, rightly handles, the word of truth, drives a straight road through the truth and refuses to be lured down pleasant but irrelevant bypaths; he ploughs a straight furrow across the field of truth; he takes each section of the truth, and fits it into its correct position, as a mason does a stone, allowing no part to usurp an undue place or an undue emphasis, and so to knock the whole structure of truth out of balance (Barclay, pp. 198–199).

This workbook is a resource for the discipline of study. Every day, if you follow the pattern suggested, you will be practicing this discipline by studying other disciplines for spiritual growth. You will be seeking and finding the truth which makes you free.

Reflecting and Recording

One of the steps involved in study is repetition. Some educators have questioned this process, contending that repetition without understanding is of little or no value. It has been proven, however, that repetition, even without understanding, does affect our inner mind, form habits, and change and shape behavior. Psychocybernetics is founded on this rationale—that we can be shaped by repeating certain affirmations. We will consider this more tomorrow. For now, accepting this first principle or step in study, spend time in memorizing Paul's word.

I appeal to you therefore, brethren, by the mercies of God, to present your bodies as a living sacrifice, holy and acceptable to God, which is your spiritual worship. Do not be conformed to this world but be transformed by the renewal of your mind, that you may prove what is the will of God, what is good and acceptable and perfect.

—Romans 12:1–2

If you have difficulty memorizing, copy the verse on a card. During this week repeat that word often every day, especially the phrase "Do not be conformed to this world but be transformed by the renewal of your mind." As a beginning practice, commit yourself to repeating it at least five times a day: when you awake in the morning, at each mealtime, and as you go to sleep at night.

Though you have already made a commitment to use this workbook, pray now that you will be strengthened in your will to "stick to it," to keep the daily discipline of using it, and that the Lord will use it for your spiritual growth and transformation.

Special Note: I included the word from William Barclay today not only to illumine the meaning of seeking the truth, but to introduce his *Daily Study Bible* as a peerless resource for studying the New Testament. This is a series of volumes on each book in the New Testament, easy to read, insightful, and practical. There is no Bible study resource I would recommend more highly.

Day Two: *We Are What We Think*

> Finally, brethren, whatever things are true, whatever things are noble, whatever things are just, whatever things are pure, whatever things are lovely, whatever things are of good report, if there is any virtue and if there is anything praiseworthy—meditate on these things.
>
> The things which you have learned and received and heard and seen in me—these do, and the God of peace will be with you.
>
> —Philippians 4:8–9, NKJV

We are what we think. The body of evidence to confirm this assertion is growing daily. Yet we each have to learn this lesson for ourselves: We are what we think. Sour dispositions create not only sick souls but also sick bodies. Feelings of worthlessness, bitter resentment, and self-pity diminish us to fragments. A possessive nature, self-indulgence, self-protectiveness, and self-centeredness shrivel the soul, create dysfunctions within us, distort perception, blur perspective, and prevent the healing we need.

The opposite of this is also true. Those who fill their minds with positive affirmations, who concentrate on the noble virtues that make life meaningful, set the stage for healing and make possible the wholeness that is God's design for all. Two thousand years before psychologists were teaching this truth, Paul discovered its power. *"Meditate on these things,"* he said—things that are noble, just, pure, lovely, of good report. We are what we think.

The discipline of study is important because how we use the dynamic power of our thinking determines whether it is Christian or not. Almost our total culture reflects a perversion of this power. The "power of positive thinking" is supposed to make us millionaires, to turn us into self-serving people bent on satisfying all our desires. Thus we have a consumer economy of indulgence and waste. It is not arrogant, I think, for Paul, as he calls people to meditate on the great virtues, to add, *"The things which you have learned and received and heard and seen in me—these do, and the God of peace will be with you"* (Phil. 4:9, NKJV). You cannot separate what Paul said from the style of his life and his passionate commitment to Christ as Lord of his life. The Christian can never use with integrity "the power of positive thinking" without keeping foremost where our thinking is to be centered. "Let this mind be in you which was also in Christ Jesus, who . . . emptied Himself by taking the form of a servant . . . humbled Himself and became obedient to the point of death" (Phil. 2:5, 7–8, NKJV).

The disciplines we pursue in this workbook are aimed at letting "the mind of Christ" grow in us.

Yesterday we mentioned the first step in study—repetition. (Are you repeating Paul's word?) Along with repetition, Richard J. Foster reminds us that there are three other steps in study: concentration, comprehension, and reflection.

Concentration centers the mind and focuses our attention. We are constantly bombarded with calls for attention, stimuli for thinking. To study, we choose to *concentrate* on a particular subject, thought, or idea.

Comprehension comes as a result of centering our attention. Throughout the time we use this workbook we will turn repeatedly to a particular discipline. We will concentrate on its meaning for a number of days in order to comprehend, to gain insight and discernment. Beyond this, at any time in your life, this will be a step in the discipline of study.

Reflection is a further step needed for study. To comprehend is to *know*. By reflection we discover the significance of what we know. Almost every day in this workbook, there will be suggestions for "reflecting and recording." These suggestions are designed to assist you in finding the significance of what you are studying for your own life.

Jesus spoke of having ears but not hearing, eyes but not seeing. John Ruskin put the point clearly:

> The greatest thing a human soul ever does in this world is *see* something, and tell what it saw in a plain way. Hundreds of people can talk for one who can think, but thousands can think for one who can see. To see clearly is poetry, prophecy and religion all in one (Ruskin, p. 286).

To see clearly, to know the significance of what we are studying, comes through reflection.

Reflecting and Recording

Let's practice. Here is a passage from *Christian Wholeness* by Thomas A. Langford:

> Two of the most popular words in present Christian vocabulary are *liberation* and *celebration*. But they are often spoken by conflicting voices and often reflect quite divergent attitudes.
>
> *Liberation* carries a deep sense of caring. It points toward the transformation of society and calls Christians to action on behalf of the dispossessed, the disenfranchised, and the neglected persons of our world.
>
> *Celebration* connotes exuberant joy. It is lighthearted. It calls persons to thanksgiving and affirmation. Celebration affirms life and catches persons up into an awareness of goodness, and an exhilaration of positive meaning.
>
> Often these two facets of experience are set in opposition. The advocate of liberation tends to seriousness, empathetically sympathizes with the brokenness of human life and carries the weight of the struggle for emancipation from structures and systems which oppress persons. The celebrant of life tends to affirm meaning already found and expresses that meaning in ecstatic movements of heart, mind, and body. At their worst, those who call for liberation are too intensely serious; and those who call for celebration are frothy and glib. At their best, those who call for liberation know that their contention in this bruised world is a part of God's contention and that God's providence underwrites their efforts. Because of this grace they rejoice. Those who call for celebration know that the good graces of life have been won by God's hard suffering and they, too, encounter debilitating pressures in life (Langford, pp. 18–19).

Read the passage again. Concentrate on it to comprehend the truth of it. Spend some time reflecting, seeking to discover its significance for you personally. Then record in a few sentences what this passage means to you, how you are perceiving life, how you are living life, and what changes you may be being called to make.

Day Three: *Persons of One Book*

> As for you, continue in what you have learned and have firmly believed, knowing from whom you learned it and how from childhood you have been acquainted with the sacred writings which are able to instruct you for salvation through faith in Christ Jesus. All scripture is inspired by God and profitable for teaching, for reproof, for correction, and for training in righteousness, that the man of God may be complete, equipped for every good work.
> —2 Timothy 3:14–17

John Wesley claimed to be "a man of one book." In a moving personal testimony, he said,

> I want to know one thing—the way to heaven; how to land safe on that happy shore. God himself has condescended to teach the way; for this very end he came from heaven. He had written it down in a book. O give me that book! At any price, give me the book of God! I have it: here is knowledge enough for me. Let me be *homo unius libri* (a man of one book). Here then I am, far from the busy ways of man. I sit down alone: only God is here. In his presence I open, I read his book; for this end, to find the way to heaven (Wesley, pp. 31–32).

For the Christian, the Bible is the final authority for belief and action. Of course we read other books and we discipline ourselves in study. But the Bible stands alone as the resource to show us how to live on earth and how to get to heaven. No discipline is more crucial for Christians than immersing ourselves in scripture. No discipline provides more power and direction for spiritual growth than scripture. For that reason, not only will we focus for a few days on this particular discipline, all the disciplines that we explore will be grounded in scripture.

Reread the scripture above and underline what you think are key words or phrases. Do that now.

What did you underline? I can imagine that among other things you underlined *teaching, reproof, correction, training in righteousness.* Let's look at these words and phrases as they call us to be "persons of one book."

Teaching. It is true that Christianity is not founded on a book but on a living person. Before we had a New Testament, we had Christians and the Christian church. But not much time passed before it was necessary for these first Christians to present this living person, Jesus, by writing his story—the Gospels. So, the fact now is that we get our firsthand account of Jesus and his teaching from the New Testament. There is no place else to get it. The Bible is irreplaceable for teaching us who God, Jesus, and the Holy Spirit are, what they have done, and what they are calling us to be.

Reproof. We normally think of reproof as finding fault and criticizing. Here it means *conviction.* Scripture convicts us, confronts and convinces us of our sin and error, but also of the pursuing grace of God, the forgiving love of Christ, and the empowering presence of the Holy Spirit.

Correction. We considered earlier Jesus' claim about knowing the truth and the truth setting us free. The correcting work of scripture is the testing of truth. We must always use our minds, dedicate them to the pursuit of truth, and truth is truth wherever we find it. The point here is that all theology, all ethical teaching, all moral codes are to be tested by the teaching of the Bible. The key to this testing is in the teaching of Jesus Christ as the scriptures present it to us. That means that isolated teachings of the Bible must be tested by the revelation of God in Jesus Christ. In him the divine Yes has been spoken.

Training in righteousness. This is the end of it all, training in righteousness, and for what purpose? "That the man of God may be complete, equipped for every good work."

John Wesley's desire "to know one thing—the way to heaven" is the deep desire of all Christians. We were made by God for that—for God and eternal rest in him. But we also study the Bible that we may live now a godly life, doing the will of God, being used by God for the salvation of others. We don't go to heaven by ourselves.

Reflecting and Recording

We have already practiced one of the ways to immerse ourselves in scripture: read a passage, underlining key words as a way to focus on meaning. Let's practice this again by underlining key words as we read this passage.

> Blessed are those whose way is blameless,
>   who walk in the law of the Lord!
> Blessed are those who keep his testimonies,
>   who seek him with their whole heart,
>   who also do no wrong, but walk in his ways!
> Thou hast commanded thy precepts to be kept diligently.
> O that my ways may be steadfast in keeping thy statutes!
> Then I shall not be put to shame,
>   having my eyes fixed on all thy commandments.

How can a young man keep his way pure?
  By guarding it according to thy word
With my whole heart I seek thee;
  let me not wander from thy commandments!
I have laid up thy word in my heart,
  that I might not sin against thee.
                            —Psalm 119:1–6; 9–11

Recalling the steps of study, repetition, concentration, and reflection, ponder the significance of this passage, using the key words and phrases for disciplining yourself with scripture.

Day Four: *More Than a Book*

When Israel was a child, I loved him,
  and out of Egypt I called my son.
The more I called them,
  the more they went from me;
they kept sacrificing to the Baals,
  and burning incense to idols.

Yet it was I who taught Ephraim to walk,
  I took them up in my arms;
  but they did not know that I healed them.
I led them with cords of compassion,
  with the bands of love,
and I became to them as one
  who eases the yoke on their jaws,
  and I bent down to them and fed them.

I am the Lord your God
  from the land of Egypt;
you know no God but me,
  and besides me there is no savior.
It was I who knew you in the wilderness,
  in the land of drought;
but when they had fed to the full,
  they were filled, and their heart was lifted up;
  therefore they forgot me.
So I will be to them like a lion,
  like a leopard I will lurk beside the way.

> I will fall upon them like a bear
>   robbed of her cubs,
> I will tear open their breast,
>   and there I will devour them like a lion,
>   as a wild beast would rend them.
>   —Hosea 11:1–4; 13:4–8

The Bible is more than a book, it is a revelation and an encounter with the living God. Reread the above passage with that fact in mind.

There are many gods, but in the Bible we encounter the living God: the God of creation (Gen. 1); the God of covenant (Gen. 12:1–7); the God of Abraham, Isaac, and Jacob (Exod. 3:1–6); the God of deliverance (Exod. 9:1–7); the God of compassion who binds us in love (Hos. 11:1–4); the God of justice and mercy (Mic. 6:6–8); the God of pursuing love who seeks us in love even to his own death in Jesus on the cross.

We serve many gods: wealth, materialism, money, greed. But the Bible says, "For what does it profit a man, to gain the whole world and forfeit his life?"(Mark 8:36).

We worship the god of sex and pleasure, but the Bible says, "Do you not know that your body is a temple of the Holy Spirit within you, which you have from God? You are not your own; you were bought with a price. So glorify God in your body"(1 Cor. 6:19–20).

We are tempted to serve the god of power, prestige, and worldly influence. However, the Bible says, "But many that are first will be last, and the last first"(Mark 10:31).

Some even serve the god of narrow, selfish, nationalism, but the Bible says God "made from one every nation of men to live on all the face of the earth" (Acts 17:26).

More than a book, the Bible is a revelation and an encounter. The Bible is also an invitation, an invitation to life. The Bible is gospel, not just Matthew, Mark, Luke, and John, but the whole of it is gospel, and gospel in invitation.

The great events of the Old Testament—creation, covenant, and exodus—all reflect gospel. The movement of God is always a movement of love toward us, a love that knows no limits. The big story of the Bible is the story of God staying with us through his grace, wooing us, loving us, seeking to restore us to our created image and bring us back into fellowship. The last verse of the Twenty-third Psalm says it well: "Surely goodness and mercy shall follow me all the days of my life; and I shall dwell in the house of the Lord for ever."

If we miss that invitation in the Old Testament, we can't miss it in the New. It is an engraved personal invitation, personally delivered by Jesus Christ. He pictured it for us in a series of parables, the lost coin, the lost sheep, and the lost son. You will find all of them in Luke 15, one of the most beloved chapters in the Bible. It has been called the "gospel in the gospel," because it contains the distilled essence of the good news Jesus came to share. Look at one of those parables, the lost sheep:

> So he told them this parable: "What man of you, having a hundred sheep, if he has lost one of them, does not leave the ninety-nine in the wilderness, and go after the one which is lost, until he finds it? And when he has found it, he lays it on his shoulders, rejoicing. And when he comes home, he calls together his friends and his neighbors, saying to them, 'Rejoice with me, for I have found my sheep which was lost.' Just so, I tell you, there will be more joy in heaven over one sinner who repents than over ninety-nine righteous persons who need no repentance."
>
> —Luke 15:3–7

The shepherd in Judea had a dangerous task. The shepherd was personally responsible for the sheep. It was all in a day's work for a shepherd to risk his life for his sheep. So Jesus took the shepherd as a model for self-sacrifice and called himself the good shepherd who lays down his life for his sheep.

The invitation is here, spelled out in the likening of God to a shepherd who never rests and risks all until every sheep is safe in the fold.

If you miss the invitation in the Old Testament and in Jesus' teaching, you can't miss it in what he does. He writes the invitation in his own blood. He goes to the cross for our sin.

Now that's difficult to comprehend, but here is a story that will help us. *The Reader's Digest* carried this beautiful story of love and devotion. A girl in a family had to have blood because of an emergency surgery situation. It was a rare form of blood and her little brother was the only one whose blood would match and would be available. They talked to the little boy about it and he agreed to give his blood to his sister. He was on the table, and they were extracting the blood. After a little while, the boy looked up at his mother and the nurse who was taking the blood, and asked, "When am I going to die?"

Do you see the point of that? Somehow the little boy had gotten the idea that giving blood to his sister so that she could live meant that he was going to die. Still he had made the decision to give her blood. It's a faint picture of what Jesus did for us on the cross.

The Bible is more than a book, it is an invitation to and gift of life. An encounter, an invitation, and more. More than a book, the Bible is a blueprint for living. This is what we considered yesterday: teaching, reproof, correction, and training for righteousness. No wonder, then, Paul says to Timothy: "You have been acquainted with the sacred writings which are able to instruct you for salvation through faith in Christ Jesus" (2 Tim. 3:15).

Reflecting and Recording

Kierkegaard suggested that "the Bible should be read as a letter from God with our personal address on it." Here is a way for doing that. Read a passage with the following three questions in mind:

1. What does this passage say? You are trying to discover meanings, to get behind the words. Reading in more than one translation helps. Rewriting a passage in your own words is very beneficial.
2. What does this passage say to *me*. Now you are beginning to *apply* the word. You are comprehending and reflecting.
3. What response and action are being called for from me? Scripture has not done its work until we have personally responded. The response may be a change of attitude, an act of mercy, accepting forgiveness, receiving comfort and peace. It may be an act of reconciliation or witnessing.

Sometime today practice reading a passage of scripture in this fashion. Be certain that you follow through with a specific response.

Day Five: *Divine Guidance*

During the past four days we have dealt in a general way with study as a discipline. Then we focused on the study of scripture. Now we turn to an even narrower focus, the matter of divine guidance and the use of scripture for guidance.

Guidance in the Christian life is a matter of grave concern and a place where discipline is sorely needed. In this decade one of the most bizarre distortions of guidance was seen in Jim Jones and the Guyana tragedy. Hundreds of people died in ceremonial suicide following the instruction of a man who claimed to be divinely guided. There are many far less dramatic examples of the distortion of guidance. A student has neglected his studies and comes to the final exam, praying for divine guidance. An athletic team prays for divine guidance to show them the way to victory. Persons who give little thought to how God would have them spend their money seek God's guidance in making money and accumulating wealth. You can add to the list—good people seeking God's guidance for questionable enterprises and even "bad" people brashly seeking divine sanction and guidance for the unrighteous direction of their lives.

So the discipline of guidance deserves careful attention. I hesitate even to open the issue with the opportunity for such a brief exploration. However the demand is upon us. If we are going to practice the Christian faith and avail ourselves of the offers of God, guidance must be considered. Note two clear facts.

One, scripture not only promises guidance, it assumes the fact of guidance throughout.

Two, Jesus promised his own guidance through the gift of the Spirit. "But now I am coming to thee; and these things I speak in the world, that they may have my joy fulfilled in themselves. I have given them thy word; and the world has hated them because they are not of the world, even as I am not of the world" (John 17:13–14).

These, then, become our primary source of guidance: scripture and Christ.

We began this workbook with the discipline of scripture. This is our primary source of guidance. Paul reminded Timothy that "all scripture is inspired by God and profitable for teaching, for reproof, for correction, and for training in righteousness, that the man of God may be complete, equipped for every good work" (2 Tim. 3:16–17). The words stand out: teaching, reproof, correction, training. We considered these aspects of the work of scripture in our lives on Day Three. This is our stance for using scripture for guidance. We don't go to the Bible now and then, open it here or there randomly, seeking guidance. We live with the Bible, submit our lives to its truth and challenge, until its cumulative influence in our lives brings us to the point where we can find light and direction for our everyday walking.

The writer to the Hebrews refers to the message of scripture as "living and active, sharper than any two-edged sword, piercing to the division of soul and spirit, of joints and marrow, and discerning the thoughts and intentions of the heart" (Heb. 4:12). Scripture as divine guidance includes judgment. It sheds the white light of God's justice and righteousness as well as the healing balm of his mercy and forgiveness.

Along with scripture we have the Holy Spirit, the living Christ, present with us to guide. He did not use the word *guidance,* but the fact and the promise of his guidance are prominent in his speaking. In his time with the disciples in the Upper Room, before his trial and crucifixion, Jesus underscored the promise of his presence and of guidance.

> I will not leave you desolate; I will come to you. Yet a little while, and the world will see me no more, but you will see me; because I live, you will live also. In that day you will know that I am in my Father, and you in me, and I in you. He who has my commandments and keeps them, he it is who loves me; and he who loves me will be loved by my Father, and I will love him and manifest myself to him. Judas (not Iscariot) said to him, "Lord, how is it that you will manifest yourself to us, and not to the world?" Jesus answered him, "If a man loves me, he will keep my word, and my Father will love him, and we will come to him and make our home with him."
>
> —John 14:18–23

> If you abide in me, and my words abide in you, ask whatever you will, and it shall be done for you.
>
> —John 15:7

> Nevertheless I tell you the truth: it is to your advantage that I go away, for if I do not go away, the Counselor will not come to you; but if I go, I will send him to you.
>
> —John 16:7

> So you have sorrow now, but I will see you again and your hearts will rejoice, and no one will take your joy from you.
>
> —John 16:22

Next week in our emphasis on prayer, we will stress a working understanding of prayer as recognizing, cultivating awareness of, and giving expression to the indwelling Christ. The big idea is that Christ indwells us Christians; the Holy Spirit is an abiding presence in our lives. To the degree that we cultivate an awareness of and are responsive to his spirit, Christ will guide us. Paul said, "For those who live according to the flesh set their minds on the things of the flesh, but those who live according to the Spirit set their minds on the things of the Spirit" (Rom. 8:5).

I wrote of the indwelling Christ as a guiding presence in my book *Alive in Christ.*

> The indwelling Christ is a guiding presence. Any one of us can call from our memory occasions when we knew for certain that we were being guided. But how much of the time do we live in anxiety, uncertain about the direction in which we should go,

immobilized by choices, impotent in the presence of opportunity because we are indecisive? We need guidance and we can't lay hold of it.

There are great decisions in life—vocation, marriage, career movement, crisis situations—when our need for guidance is vividly pronounced. But what plagues us most and drains us of so much energy are the intersections upon which we come every day, and when we have to choose which way to go. To be sure, we need guidance at the major intersections of our lives, but we need it also at the little crossings and turnings of which our lives primarily consist. My plea is that we see guidance not as episodic, but as an ongoing dynamic which shapes our beings and thus determines decisions and directions.

The guidance of the indwelling Christ is consistent and ongoing. This does not mean that there are not specific times when we seek explicit guidance in particular situations. It does mean that through prayer and other spiritual disciplines we seek to cultivate the awareness of the indwelling Christ to the point that we are delivered from a frantic disposition of mind and heart in the face of decision. We do not come "cold turkey" to a minor or a major crisis. We have the inner sense of Christ's presence. Calling upon that presence, direction is often so clear that the right decision does not even require deciding (Dunnam, *Alive in Christ*, p. 84).

Reflecting and Recording

In *The Lower Levels of Prayer,* George S. Stewart says there are three fundamental conditions which we must meet to receive divine guidance (pp. 166–167).

1. We must be traveling the same road as our guide.
2. We must habitually seek guidance and watch for it.
3. We must habitually follow the guidance given.

We will look at these again tomorrow. For now assess your practice of seeking guidance.

First, recall an experience in which you felt divinely guided. Record that experience here.

Did the guidance come either through scripture or from the living Christ through prayer? If neither of these, how?

Examine your daily life in light of the conditions for receiving guidance. How are these conditions being met in your life?

Pray for guidance in pursuing a discipline of guidance.

Day Six: *Conditions as Disciplines*

Yesterday we stated three conditions that, according to George Stewart, must be met to receive divine guidance.

1. We must be traveling the same road as our guide.
2. We must habitually seek guidance and watch for it.
3. We must habitually follow the guidance given.

These conditions may, in fact, become ongoing disciplines. We practice them to enhance divine guidance in our lives. Let's focus on the conditions for receiving guidance as disciplines for spiritual growth. Look at them in this fashion.

The first condition, that we must be traveling the same road as our guide, needs no comment except a word about the mercy and grace of God for those who don't follow the guide. Dr. Stewart said it well in *The Lower Levels of Prayer:*

> There is much Divine Guidance in lives that do not observe these conditions, restraining and saving while men are on the wrong road and following the wrong guide. There is light that comes to those who are not seeking and to those who are living in disobedience. This is the mercy of God which is ever seeking men in their wandering, and in pity saving and delivering (Stewart, p. 169).

John Wesley would call this *prevenient grace*—God going before, loving, leading, constraining, restraining, in every way seeking to move in a person's life until that person yields to grace. So we affirm that sort of guidance for all. Yet, the truth remains: for a "guided life" we must walk in the same way as our Guide.

Second, we must habitually seek guidance and watch for it. Occasional guidance may come to those who sporadically seek, but ongoing guidance—guidance that is not episodic and crisis oriented— comes to those who habitually seek. Jesus sounded the requirement: Ask, seek, knock. He also offered the reward: "For every one who asks receives, and he who seeks finds, and to him who knocks it will be opened"(Luke 11:10).

Think: Is there anything that pleases God more than a life yielded to him? God is always seeking us; that is his nature—seeking love. It takes open eyes and minds and hearts longing for and sensitive to his coming to perceive the guidance God continually offers.

Third, habitually follow the guidance given. *Obedience* is the added essential ingredient here.

Unfortunately we think of obedience as an issue only in huge events and at the crucial intersections of our lives. Not so. Obedience in the mundane and daily affairs of life, even the "little" things makes obedience possible at the "big" times. Responding to the promptings of kindness and love which the Spirit initiates; *doing the word* as we discover that word in scripture even if it means as simple an act as taking a meal to a sick person in our neighborhood; *exercising the indwelling Christ,* visiting widows and orphans, clothing the naked, sending a sacrificial offering to feed starving children—these are examples of daily obedience to God.

The more we exercise obedience the clearer will be our perceptions, and guidance will become more and more real in our lives. When we are in fellowship with Christ through scripture and disciplined prayer, we will experience the leading of the Holy Spirit. Quenching that Spirit is sin. Such resistance of the Spirit dulls our sensitivity to the leading of the Spirit and stops our ears to the Spirit's voice. In fellowship with Christ, we will know his striving within us. Clarifying the leadings of the Spirit, acting upon them habitually is a discipline for spiritual growth that most of us rather desperately need.

Reflecting and Recording

Assuming that we are Christian, seeking to walk with Christ, our guide, ponder and respond to these questions:

Do you habitually seek guidance and watch for it? Record here your most recent experience of seeking guidance.

Do you find yourself praying for guidance, but then in the days that follow failing to watch for it and possibly missing it?

Do you habitually follow the guidance given? List briefly here, just enough to clarify them in your mind, two or three occasions when you followed guidance you received.

Go back to these experiences and put a date on each one. What do these dates say about ongoing guidance in your life?

Can you recall instances when you did not follow guidance received? Record up to three instances here.

Close this period now by thinking about whether you desire more divine guidance in your life, why you are not currently experiencing the guidance you need and want, and what you are going to do to discipline yourself in receiving guidance.

What most of us need is not *desire* for guidance but *will*—the will to discipline ourselves and to be obedient. Pray for will.

Day Seven: *Other Channels*

Two days ago we considered the fact that divine guidance comes primarily from scripture and from the living Christ through prayer. Let's look at some other channels for guidance.

First, people. We are guided by other persons. It is one of my strong convictions and thrilling experiences that as we come alive in Christ, we can be Christ to and/or receive Christ from every person we meet. As I noted in *Alive in Christ:*

> Often I will begin a retreat by having persons share a love greeting. I ask them to select some one they don't know very well or not at all, get the person's first name, and exchange a greeting in this fashion. In pairs, they stand facing each other, holding both hands of each other, looking each other directly in the eye, and saying, "Mary, the love of Jesus in me greets the love of Jesus in you, and brings us together in the name of the Father, the Son, and the Holy Spirit." Then the other person shares the same greeting. I instruct them ahead of time to sit quietly after each has shared the greeting, without any comment, reflecting on what they are feeling. It is amazing how the mood changes. It is not unusual to see tears in people's eyes and have persons witness to a vivid awareness of the presence of Christ.
>
> To be sure, this is in a special setting, but it at least suggests an ever-present possibility. John A. T. Robinson said, "The Christian cannot look into a human face without seeing Jesus and cannot look into Jesus' face without seeing God." The more we cultivate our awareness of the indwelling Christ, the more we resonate to his aliveness in others and discern his guidance through them. Also, the more sensitive we are to his presence, the more perceptive we are to the pain and need of others which present calls to our lives (Dunnam, *Alive in Christ,* pp. 86–87).

When Christ said, "Ye are the light of the world," he affirmed this principle of guidance. How important is it that we know ourselves as "light" by which others walk, and how crucial it is to have a few people upon whom we depend as light.

A word about corporate guidance is called for here. The case for corporate guidance is clear in scripture—underscored over and over again in the Old Testament by God's choice of *a people*, Israel, to be the channel of his covenant and grace for all people. In the New Testament the word is even more pronounced and given to all. "Again I say to you, if two of you agree on earth about anything they ask, it will be done for them by my Father in heaven. For where two or three are gathered in my name, there am I in the midst of them" (Matt. 18:19–20).

Jesus gives the promise that when people gather in his name, are yielded to his spirit, he will speak; his guidance will be discerned. This corporate setting for receiving the Holy Spirit is radiantly, even radically, portrayed in the Book of Acts. Responding to the last words of Jesus to tarry in Jerusalem, they waited *together*. The Spirit came and the outcome was astounding.

> And all who believed were together and had all things in common; and they sold their possessions and goods and distributed them to all, as any had need. And day by day, attending the temple together and breaking bread in their homes, they partook of food with glad and generous hearts, praising God and having favor with all the people. And the Lord added to their number day by day those who were being saved.
>
> —Acts 2:44–47

> Now the company of those who believed were of one heart and soul, and no one said that any of the things which he possessed was his own, but they had everything in common. And with great power the apostles gave their testimony to the resurrection of the Lord Jesus, and great grace was upon them all. There was not a needy person among them, for as many as were possessors of lands or houses sold them, and brought the proceeds of what was sold and laid it at the apostles' feet; and distribution was made to each as any had need.
>
> —Acts 4:32–35

Elton Trueblood has called us to be what the New Testament church was, an incendiary fellowship. Corporate guidance was an identifying mark of this fellowship. Here is a marvelous illustration of it.

> Now in the church at Antioch there were prophets and teachers, Barnabas, Simeon who was called Niger, Lucius of Cyrene,

Manaen a member of the court of Herod the tetrarch, and Saul. While they were worshiping the Lord and fasting, the Holy Spirit said, "Set apart for me Barnabas and Saul for the work to which I have called them." Then after fasting and praying they laid their hands on them and sent them off.

—Acts 13:1–3

Note that the disciplines of worship, prayer, and fasting were included in this experience. It is rather clear that all congregations should be settings where corporate guidance is received and responded to. As people worship and pray together, share the sacraments, and hear the word preached, guidance comes. But a more specific focus is needed. Most of us need a small group, a few persons with whom we covenant in prayer, study, sharing, fasting perhaps, and confession. In this intimate setting, genuinely seeking the Lord's will and supporting one another in our walks, we will hear the Lord clearly; and guidance will come. Also, it is in such a relationship that we may test the personal guidance we have received in private through scripture and prayer. A way to begin this is to invite a few others to join you in using this workbook and gathering weekly to share.

Space allows only mentioning other channels of guidance: imagination, emotion, instincts, conscience, reason, common sense, and sense of duty. Dr. Stewart again speaks a clear word here.

It is a strange thing that the primitive instincts, hunger and thirst, love and passion and social instincts should be so much ignored in religious books, except as voices which misguide. Give them a place, these fundamental and overwhelming urges of flesh and spirit, not of flesh alone. Very corruptible, yes! So is conscience, so is the sense of duty—to what atrocities have these led men! So is the whole range of reason and judgment and emotion and imagination. Very corruptible. They all need to be brought into submission to Christ if they are not to lead us wrong, but asked humbly, each has its own special light and guidance to yield (Stewart, pp. 179–180).

Reflecting and Recording

To verify the channels of guidance in your life recall a recent experience in which you made a clear decision, went in a certain way, or initiated a change in your life. Record that here.

Now, reflect on how you came to your final point of judgment or decision. Did you pray? What happened?

Was scripture involved?

Did you have a sense of direct, specific divine guidance—a word from the Lord? How did it come?

Did guidance come through emotion? instinct? imagination? conscience? a sense ot duty? reason? common sense?

Select a couple of the channels *not* a part of the guidance experience you have just been reflecting on. List them.

1. _____

2. _____

See if you can recall experiences in which you were guided through these channels. Record those in the spaces provided.

Close your time by reflecting upon how you can use these channels through which guidance comes with the three disciplines for guidance: (1) travel the same road as the guide, (2) habitually seek guidance and watch for it, (3) habitually follow the guidance given.

Group Meeting for Week One

Introduction

These group sessions will be most meaningful as they reflect the experience of all the participants. This guide is simply an effort to facilitate personal sharing. Therefore, do not be rigid in following these suggestions. The leader, especially, should seek to be sensitive to what is going on in the lives of the participants and to focus the group sharing on those experiences. Ideas are important. We should wrestle with new ideas as well as with ideas with which we disagree. It is important, however, that the group meeting not become a debate about ideas. The emphasis should be on persons—experiences, feelings, and meaning.

As the group comes to the place where all can share honestly and openly what is happening in their lives, the more meaningful the experience will be. This does not mean sharing only the good or positive; share also the struggles, the difficulties, the negatives.

Discipline is not easy; it is deceptive to pretend it is. Don't be afraid to share your questions, reservations, and "dry periods" as well as that in which you find meaning.

Sharing Together

1. You may begin your time together by allowing time for each person in the group to share his or her most meaningful day with the workbook this week. The leader should begin this sharing. Tell why that particular day was so meaningful.

2. Now share your most difficult day. Tell what you experienced and why it was so difficult.

3. Ask each person in the group to name the one book, apart from the Bible, which he or she has read and would recommend as valuable to others. In a brief sentence or two, share why the book was important. Persons in the group may wish to write the titles down for future reference.

4. Ask if anyone in the group would like to share a way of reading the Bible that may be helpful to others.

5. Let each person in the group who will share his or her most meaningful experience of guidance, with the group taking special note of how the guidance came.

Praying Together

Corporate prayer is one of the great blessings of Christian community. Next week we will focus on the discipline of prayer, but this is personal. There is power in corporate prayer, and it is important that this dimension be included in our shared pilgrimage.

It is also important that you feel comfortable in this and that no pressure be placed on anyone to pray aloud. *Silent* corporate prayer is as vital and meaningful as verbal corporate prayer. Hopefully, the group will spend at least some time at each group meeting in corporate prayer.

God does not need to hear our verbal words to hear our prayers. Silence, where thinking is centered and attention is focused, may provide our deepest periods of prayer. There is power, however, in a community on a common journey verbalizing their thoughts and feelings to God in the presence of their fellow pilgrims.

Verbal prayers should be offered spontaneously as a person chooses to pray aloud—not "let's go around the circle now, and each one pray."

Suggestions for this "praying together" time will be given each week. The leader for the week should regard these only as suggestions. What is happening in the meeting—the mood, the needs that are expressed, the timing—should determine the direction of the group praying together. Here are some possibilities for this closing period.

1. Let the group think back over the sharing that has taken place during this session. What personal needs or concerns came out of the sharing? Begin to speak these aloud—any person verbalizing a need or a concern that has been expressed. Don't hesitate to mention a concern that you may have picked up from another, i.e., "Mary isn't able to be with us this week because her son is in the hospital. Let's pray for her son and for her."

It will be helpful for each person to make notes of the concerns and needs that are mentioned. Enter deliberately into a period of silence. Let the leader verbalize each of these needs successively, allowing for a brief period following each so that persons in the group may center their attention and focus their prayers on the person, need, or concern mentioned. All of this will be in silence as each person prays in *his* or *her own way.*

2. Let the leader close this time of sharing and silent prayer by asking the group to share in a prayer liturgy. The leader will call the name of each person in the group, after which the group will say, "Lord, bless him/her" as they focus their eyes on that person. Let the person whose name is called look at each person in the room to catch their eye and receive their "look" of blessing as well as their word. When this is done, the leader calls the next name, until all are called "blessed" and looked at with a blessing. Then the leader may simply say, "Amen."

Note: If someone in the group has an instant camera, bring it to the group meeting next week, prepared to take a picture of each person in the group to be used as an aid to prayer.

Prayer

Day One: *To Know That We Are Known and Loved by God*

> Seek the Lord while he may be found,
>   call upon him while he is near;
> let the wicked forsake his way,
>   and the unrighteous man his thoughts;
> let him return to the Lord, that he
>   may have mercy on him,
>   and to our God, for he will abundantly pardon.
> For my thoughts are not your thoughts,
>   neither are your ways my ways, says the Lord.
> For as the heavens are higher than the earth,
>   so are my ways higher than your ways
>   and my thoughts than your thoughts.
>   —Isaiah 55:6–9

I have written three books on prayer, two of them predecessors in this workbook series: *The Workbook of Living Prayer* and *The Workbook of Intercessory Prayer.* As I planned this workbook on spiritual disciplines, I knew that no resource of this kind could be complete without an emphasis on prayer. But what would I provide for a one-week focus that I had not done in the combined fourteen weeks of the two previous workbooks?

Naturally, if you have not done so, I invite you to use the previous workbooks as a resource for growing in a life of prayer. Even so, prayer has such an expansive range of expression, is so pivotal to our spiritual growth, and is so mysterious, rich, and intimately personal, that its depths could not be plumbed in a dozen books, much less three. So I dedicate myself to provide in this week's focus some insight and guidance for you to enrich your practice of prayer as a discipline for spiritual growth.

In *Yes to God,* Alan Ecclestone has expressed the primary function of prayer in this fashion: "Prayer remains the means by which we grope our way towards that which alone can satisfy the profoundest need of our human life: to know that we are known and loved by God." Christian prayer is many things, and certainly has many facets, but undergirding them all is this thirsting for the awareness of a loving God.

Love—longing to be loved, but also *longing love*—is at the heart of prayer. A life of prayer is a life of desire, of yearning, of hunger, of thirst. The Book of Psalms is full of expressions of this life.

> O God, thou art my God, I seek thee,
>   my soul thirsts for thee;
>   my flesh faints for thee,
>   as in a dry and weary land where no water is.
>   —Psalm 63:1

> I stretch out my hands to thee;
>   my soul thirsts for thee like a parched land.

> Make haste to answer me, O Lord!
>   My spirit fails!
> Hide not thy face from me,
>   lest I be like those who go down to the Pit.
> Let me hear in the morning of thy steadfast love,
>   for in thee I put my trust.
> Teach me the way I should go,
>   for to thee I lift up my soul.
>   —Psalm 143:6–8

> As a hart longs for flowing streams,
>   so longs my soul for thee, O God.
> My soul thirsts for God, for the living God.
> When shall I come and behold the face of God?
>   —Psalm 42:1–2

While this hungering and thirsting are a necessary condition of attention to God, it is not sufficient. As Douglas Steere reminds us:

> The sufficiency is supplied by the redemptive life of the living God, poured out in Jesus Christ, and poured out in each moment here and now. The life of sanctity is a mad response to the initiative of the mad love of God that has come into a realization that God holds it in the utter consuming, transforming, energizing irradiation of His costly love (Steere, p. 188).

Meister Eckhart expresses it with dramatic clarity:

> God is foolishly in love with us. It seems He has forgotten heaven and earth and deity; his entire business seems to be with me alone, to give me everything to comfort me; he gives it to me suddenly. He gives it to me wholly, he gives it to me perfect, he gives it all the time, and he gives it to all creatures (Steere, p. 188).

The word with which we began this reflection is from Chapter 55 of Isaiah. The prophet began the chapter with the thrilling invitation, "Ho, everyone who thirsts, come to the waters."

We seek the Lord because he can be found. We thirst because he alone can and does cool our parched spiritual tongues. We hunger because he offers himself as the bread of life which alone can nourish our famished souls. Our most profound need—to know that we are known and loved by God—drives us to prayer. Yet, prayer is more than a groping toward this awareness. It is not only longing to be loved, it is *longing love*—love that longs to be whole, to be fully expressive, to be in communion with God who first loved us.

Reflecting and Recording

Recall a specific experience or a particular time frame when you were aware of being known and loved by God. Describe that experience in a brief paragraph.

Most of us, I think, are not always aware of being known and loved by God. It seems to be an experience that comes and goes. Also, many persons have experiences of being separated from God, not known and loved by God. There are even those times when some of us feel that God does not love us; in fact, there may come the experience of feeling that God is against us. Get in touch with an experience when you felt separated, not known, not loved, maybe even that God was against you. Describe that experience.

These kinds of feelings—both of being and not being loved and known—underscore the need for discipline in our prayers. Using this workbook will assist us in that. Close your time now with a prayer of thanksgiving for the fact that you are known and loved by God.

Day Two: *In the Deeps of Our Souls Attached to God*

Sketching for a group of ministers what their calling demanded, Evelyn Underhill in *Concerning the Inner Life* described a person of prayer as one "who deliberately wills and steadily desires" that his or her interactions with God and other people be controlled entirely by God. Such people have developed their spiritual sense to the point that their "supernatural environment is more real and solid" to them than their natural environment. Persons of prayer do not necessarily recite a given number of prayers or follow a specific ritual. They are, rather, children of God, who know themselves to be in the deeps of their souls "attached to God... wholly and entirely guided by the Creative Spirit" in their prayers and work.

Underhill believed that all Christians begin with the opportunity for this apostolic life, but only a few develop it. Laypersons know immediately whether clergy have developed it or not. There is nothing you can do for other people or for God, according to Underhill, which is more important than "the achievement of that spiritual temper and attitude."

Focus on the bold affirmation that persons of prayer are children of God who are and know themselves to be in the deeps of their souls "attached to God and . . . wholly and entirely guided by the Creative Spirit" in their prayers and work. This builds on our reflection yesterday. Prayer is the movement of God to persons and persons to God. It is the rhythm of encounter and response. In this sense all Christian life is prayer.

For this to be so, however, we must be disciplined in regular times and concentration points in prayer. These specific times and practices of prayer provide a framework for cultivating a life which becomes all prayer. So, in this week of emphasis on prayer as a discipline for spiritual growth, we will focus on prayer as a living encounter with the living God, seeking as Paul admonished us in First Thessalonians 5:17 "to pray without ceasing" (KJV)—to achieve a continuous state of recollection and awareness of the presence of God.

The center and dynamic for such praying is the living Christ. In the mystery of the incarnation, God coming to us in Jesus, it is possible for us to see and know God in a continuous state of recollection and awareness. In my book *Alive in Christ,* I explored the bold claim that the indwelling Christ is to be the shaping power of our lives. To be alive in Christ is the dynamic process of our spiritual formation. I defined spiritual formation as "that dynamic process of receiving through faith and appropriating through commitment, discipline, and action, the living Christ into our own life to the end that our life will conform to, and manifest the reality of Christ's presence in the world" (p. 26).

In this understanding, one form and function of prayer is recognizing, cultivating awareness of, and giving expression to the indwelling Christ. This is an expression of contemplative prayer.

Most of the traditional and classic writing on contemplation leaves the impression that such prayer is very special, the highest form of prayer, and very difficult. Thus the common idea that contemplation, or contemplative prayer, is not for ordinary people. This is an unfortunate understanding, and not so. Basically contemplative prayer is prayer in which we give God our total attention. We attentively look at God. But more, it is a life stance. Anthony Bloom, in a personal conversation, shared with me the essence of his understanding of contemplation. His is a very practical insight which all can appropriate. Contemplation is "a way of relating to God, to yourself, to the surrounding situation in an attentive, thoughtful manner. In religious terms it may be called waiting on God. It's simply listening and looking in order to hear and understand . . . pondering, thinking deeply, waiting until one has understood in order to act. Then action is much more efficient, less hasty, and filled, probably, with some amount of divine wisdom.''

Again, the center of such praying and living is Christ. To give our attention to God, to look at God (since nobody can see God and live), we look at Jesus Christ. How often we become impatient, like Philip, who responded to Jesus' word about the Father. Do you recall that exchange?

> Jesus said to him, "I am the way, and the truth, and the life; no one comes to the Father, but by me. If you had known me, you would have known my Father also; henceforth you know him and have seen him." Philip said to him, "Lord, show us the Father, and we shall be satisfied." Jesus said to him, "Have I been with you so long, and yet you do not know me, Philip? He who has seen me has seen the Father; how can you say, 'Show us the Father'? Do you not believe that I am in the Father and the Father in me? The words that I say to you I do not speak on my own authority; but the Father who dwells in me does his works. Believe me that I am in the Father and the Father in me; or else believe me for the sake of the works themselves."
>
> —John 14:6–11

Here the great mystery of the incarnation serves us in our praying. The incarnation makes it possible for us to see God in and through Jesus Christ. "He who has seen me has seen the Father," Jesus said (John 14:9). Christ is the image of God. We know that God is a loving Father by looking at his Son.

Return now to the earlier proposition: *One form and function of prayer is recognizing, cultivating awareness of, and giving expression to the indwelling Christ.*

Reflecting and Recording

Get in touch with the living Christ by gazing at this scriptural portrait of him.

> While he was in one of the cities, there came a man full of leprosy; and when he saw Jesus, he fell on his face and besought him, "Lord, if you will, you can make me clean." And he stretched out his hand, and touched him, saying, "I will; be clean." And immediately the leprosy left him.
>
> —Luke 5:12–13

Write your feelings about Jesus as you see him in this incident.

Pray now that this understanding and awareness of Christ will flavor all that you do during this day.

Day Three: *Creating a Welcome for God and Responding to God's Welcome*

O Lord, our Lord,
  how majestic is thy name in all the earth!
Thou whose glory above the heavens is chanted
  by the mouth of babes and infants,
thou hast founded a bulwark because of thy foes,
  to still the enemy and the avenger.

When I look at thy heavens, the work of thy fingers,
  the moon and the stars which thou has established;
what is man that thou art mindful of him,
  and the son of man that thou dost care for him?

Yet thou hast made him little less than God,
  and dost crown him with glory and honor.
Thou hast given him dominion over the works of thy hands;
  thou hast put all things under his feet,
all sheep and oxen,
  and also the beasts of the field,
the birds of the air, and the fish of the sea,
  whatever passes along the paths of the sea.

O Lord, our Lord,
  how majestic is thy name in all the earth!

—Psalm 8

Alan Watts showed the frantic futility of our moving around by a comparison to royalty. A king and a queen are the center of "where it's at," so they move with easy, royal bearing. They have no place to "get." They have already "arrived."

Triggered by that image, Tilden Edwards says:

> Looking deeply at our lineage, we see that we are of the highest royal line: the royal image of God is in us—covered over, but indestructibly there. We need rush nowhere else to get it. We mainly need to attentively relax and dissolve the amnesia that obscures our true identity. . . . When we know who we really are, life loses false striving and gains simple presence (Edwards, p. 74).

The psalmist celebrated our royal lineage as "little less than God, (crowned) with glory and honor." The celebration is in an attitude of surprise, awe, amazement that God is mindful of us creatures, that God cares for us and gives us dominion. The psalm celebration is a prayer which *creates a welcome for God and response to God's welcome.*

This is akin to the double movement we considered on Day One of this week: longing to be loved and longing love.

The key to welcoming God and responding to God's welcome is attitude. Three ingredients are essential: openness, stillness, and waiting.

- By openness I mean expectancy and readiness. We expect to be with God; we are ready for God to be with us however he pleases.
- By stillness I mean settling down in quietness, pulling in the reigns of our thoughts and feelings to seek a centeredness—giving our attention to God.
- By waiting I mean not anticipating, not forcing. We wait to welcome the One we trust will appear.

Here is a prayer pattern that will facilitate this openness, stillness, waiting. It is adapted from *Scala Claustralium* (The Ladder of Monks) and includes four steps. The symbol for this prayer pattern is a ladder, each four steps representing a rung on the ladder. The steps are reading, meditation, prayer, communion or contemplation.

Preparation must be made for the most rewarding experience: a quiet place, preselected reading, adequate time reserved for this welcoming and being welcomed by God.

Reading. You may use some other devotional resource, but scripture is really the primary source for our life and prayer. If you are beginning to pray in this fashion select a Gospel first. I would suggest

Mark or John. Approach the scripture not as a textbook, not with the intention of acquiring knowledge, but as a word that God is going to speak to you. Resist the urge to "plow through" and move on. You do not even have to read a set number of verses or a chapter. Move slowly, with a listening heart, until you come to something that "speaks to you," that invites your further attention. Stop there because you have come to the place for a second step.

Meditation. Some understand meditation as a passive emptying of the mind, a dissolving of our thoughts until we are at one with spirit; some Eastern concepts of meditation would say "at one with nothingness."

There is value in meditation that is an emptying of the mind and a centering that rests us in the stillness that is at the heart of our hearts. The meditation that is a step in this prayer experience is not that. It is not passive but active. In a pamphlet entitled *A Pattern for Christian Prayer,* Stephen V. Sprinkle puts it thus:

> Love has drawn you to deeper consideration of a phrase of Scripture. Meditation is the consideration of the heart; it is to the reading of Scripture what the taste buds are to eating. Meditation allows us to savor the Scripture to which we have been drawn. "Taste and see that the Lord is good," advises the Psalmist, and meditation is the means by which the flavor of God's Word is derived. There is no need to analyze or pick apart what is read. Rather than breaking verses down into understandable pieces for teaching or preaching, meditation makes us a part of the Word and the Word a part of us.

Such active meditation or tasting the word moves us beyond the word to God, to Christ the living Word. The time may be two, three, or five minutes, maybe longer, but the heart not the clock is your time keeper. Then comes step three.

Prayer. Reading and meditation are preludes to prayer as we use this pattern. Prayer, in this experience, is the complete focusing of our thoughts and our total being on what we wish to share with God. For most of us words will probably be involved. We offer our thanks, we confess our sins and failures, we affirm our faith, we make our petitions, we intercede for others, we listen to God and respond to God's call with the commitment of our lives. Then comes the final step.

Communion or *contemplation.* Now we simply wait in love and silence, resting in the fact that we belong to God and that we desire the Holy Spirit to act in the deepest recesses of our hearts and minds. At its most vivid expression, this time is brief and exquisitely simple, as we know divine love permeating our beings. We have welcomed God and in this moment God welcomes us.

Reflecting and Recording

Now, or sometime during the day, use this pattern. Use Psalm 8 with which we began this session as your reading. Set aside a time tomorrow, other than the time you are working with this workbook material, when you will use the pattern again. Begin with the first chapter of the Gospel of John as your reading.

Day Four: *Contemplative Prayer as Awareness of Christ*

It is interesting that the apostle Paul doesn't talk about prayer as a part of life but as all of life. For him, prayer is not something that we should *not forget,* not something that we should practice regularly, it is our ongoing concern; therefore we are to pray unceasingly. Here are his words:

> Pray constantly, give thanks in all circumstances; for this is the will of God in Christ Jesus for you.
> —1 Thessalonians 5:17–18

> We give thanks to God always for you all, constantly mentioning you in our prayers, remembering you before our God.
> —1 Thessalonians 1:2–3

> We pray for you constantly, that God will think you worthy of this calling.
> —2 Thessalonians 1:11, Phillips

> Without ceasing I mention you always in my prayers.
> —Romans 1:9

Repeatedly, the Greek terms, *pantote* (always) and *adialeiptos* (without interruption) are used by Paul in his letters. There is a fervor here that disallows partial or piecemeal commitment. Not a part but all of our life is what prayer is about.

On Day Two of this week we began a consideration of one way to respond to Paul's call to pray without ceasing, that is to cultivate an awareness of the living Christ. This is a helpful understanding of contemplative prayer; awareness of Christ. I reiterate, Christ is the image of God. Living in awareness of Christ is living with God, thus praying unceasingly.

But how? That is the question.

Henri Nouwen has provided a very helpful clue by connecting unceasing thoughts with unceasing prayer.

We are thinking beings. The most common expression of thinking is what we commonly label *reflection*. This is a conscious mental consideration of ideas, images, emotions, experiences. We reflect by decision, by will power and concentrated effort. Reflection is intentional.

But there is also thinking that is not deliberate. We find ourselves "thinking" without having decided to do so. I sat down to write today and before I got into the flow, I found myself thinking about being on the beach in Southern California. Where did that thought come from? Maybe from the fact that a couple of days ago I received an invitation to speak in San Clemente. But it doesn't require that sort of stimulation or connection. More often than not, it just happens. We can't control it, and that's even a bit frightening. As often as not our thoughts are uncontrolled and uncontrollable.

Think now—there is yet another layer of thinking, as Nouwen reminds us,

> deeper than our reflective moments and our uncontrolled mental wanderings. They also reach into our sleeping hours. We might wake up in the middle of the night and find ourselves part of a frightening car race, a delicious banquet, or a heavenly choir. Sometimes we are able to give a detailed account of all the things that happened to us in our dreams: what we heard as well as what we said. Sometimes we remember only the final moment of our dream, and sometimes we are left with only a vague fear or an undefined joy. We know that much is going on during our sleep, of which, only occasionally, we catch bits and pieces. Careful brain-wave studies have shown that our mind is always active during sleep; we are always dreaming even when we have no recollection of its occurrence or its content. And, although we might tend to regard our thought processes during our night's sleep as insignificant in comparison with our reflections or our undirected mental wanderings, we should not forget that for many people dreams proved to be the main source of knowing. The patriach Jacob heard God's call when he saw the angels going up and down a ladder; in the Old Testament Joseph was deported to Egypt because he irritated his brothers with his visions of sheaves, sun, moon, and stars bowing to him; and in the New Testament Joseph fled to Egypt after he had seen an angel warning him of Herod. And in our century, apparently so far from biblical times, we find Sigmund Freud and Carl Jung informing us that our dreams will tell us our truth (Nouwen, p. 67–68).

Now the point of all this is to make the case for converting the unceasing thinking in which as humans we are all involved into unceasing prayer. To be sure, it will be a lifetime project, but I can't think of a more rewarding and enriching lifetime project—turning our whole life into a prayer. All the disciplines for spiritual growth will contribute to this, but the discipline of prayer is to specifically serve this purpose.

We can pray scripture in a way that will take us along the road to unceasing prayer. The big idea is that we have a time (preferably each day) when we deliberately live with scripture and focus our attention on Christ. We can then cultivate an awareness of his presence, reflect upon his person and character, intently listen to him so that he becomes such a part of our being that his presence permeates consciously and unconsciously the rest of our day.

Reflecting and Recording

As we did yesterday, let's concentrate on Jesus as we see him in scripture.

> After he had ended all his sayings in the hearings of the people he entered Capernaum. Now a centurion had a slave who was dear to him, who was sick and at the point of death. When he heard of Jesus, he sent to him elders of the Jews, asking him to come and heal his slave. And when they came to Jesus, they besought him earnestly, saying, "He is worthy to have you do this for him, for he loves our nation, and he built us our synagogue." And Jesus went with them. When he was not far from the house, the centurion sent friends to him, saying to him, "Lord, do not trouble yourself, for I am not worthy to have you come under my roof; therefore I did not presume to come to you. But say the word, and let my servant be healed. For I am a man set under authority, with soldiers under me; and I say to one, 'Go,' and he goes; and to another, 'Come,' and he comes; and to my slave, 'Do this,' and he does it." When Jesus heard this he marveled at him, and turned and said to the multitude that followed him, "I tell you, not even in Israel have I found such faith." And when those who had been sent returned to the house, they found the slave well.
>
> —Luke 7:1–10

Make some notes about how you see Jesus in this incident. Pay attention to how the elders of the Jews saw the centurion, how the centurion saw Jesus, and how Jesus responded to it all.

Commit yourself now to carry with you into the day the faith of the centurion and the awareness of Jesus responding to faith and to need wherever he finds it. Continue your praying by consciously bringing all your concerns into your fresh awareness of Christ.

Day Five: *Bringing Our Thoughts Out of the Closet*

Converting our unceasing thoughts into unceasing prayer means bringing our thoughts "out of the closet."

Most of us have experienced disturbing uneasiness, even fear, stemming from "wild" thoughts that enter our minds, the sexual lust that comes to consciousness, the desire to hurt another, the unaccounted-for-wish that ill might come to us or to another, the fantasy to be completely free of any responsibility and any relationship, the fantasy of "doom" that something awful and destructive is going to happen, the desire selfishly to protect for yourself—to hide or hoard—money or some gift or "goodie" that has come to you.

Stop for a few minutes and see if you can identify thoughts that you have had during the past week or two that made you uneasy or fearful. Record those here.

Some of us have a pattern of recurring thoughts or dreams that upset us, make us fearful, or leave us with painful feelings of guilt. Is that true with you? Think about it and record such recurring thoughts or dreams here. Write enough to clarify your own perception of what the thoughts and dreams are.

Deliberately now, offer the thoughts and feelings you have written in these two exercises to God. This isn't to say that God doesn't already know; God does. But prayer is dialogue. It is our conscious sharing with God. So do that now.

Even from this brief and limited experience we can begin to sense that clarity of understanding and change of feeling can take place when we bring our thoughts out of the closet.

Next week we will consider confession as a discipline of spiritual growth. Prayer is integral to that process. However, we must not confuse prayer with introspection. Henri Nouwen rightly reminds us that

> introspection means to look inward, to enter into the complex network of our mental processes in search of some inner logic or some elucidating connections. Introspection results from the desire to know ourselves better and to become more familiar with our own interiority. Although introspection has a positive role in our thought processes, the danger is that it can entangle us in the labyrinth of our own ideas, feelings, and emotions and lead us to an increasing self-preoccupation. Introspection can cause paralyzing worries or unproductive self-gratification. Introspection can also create "moodiness." This "moodiness' is a very widespread phenomenon in our society. It betrays our great concern with ourselves and undue sensitivity to how we feel or think. It makes us experience life as a constant fluctuation between "feeling high" and "feeling low," between "bad days" and "good days," and thus becomes a form of narcissism.
>
> Prayer is not introspection. It is not a scrupulous, inward-looking analysis of our own thoughts and feelings but a careful attentiveness to him who invites us to an unceasing conversation. Prayer is the presentation of all thoughts—reflective thoughts as well as daydreams and night dreams—to our loving Father so that he can see them and respond to them with his divine compassion. Prayer is the joyful affirmation that God knows our minds and hearts and that nothing is hidden from him. It is saying with Psalm 138* (Grail translation, Paulist Press):

> O Lord, you search me and you know me,
> you know my resting and my rising,
> you discern my purpose from afar.
> You mark when I walk or lie down,
> all my ways lie open to you [1–3].
> O search me, God, and know my heart.
> O test me and know my thoughts.
> See that I follow not the wrong path
> and lead me in the path of life eternal [23–24].

(Nouwen, p. 72–73)

*Editor's Note: This is Psalm 139 in many other translations of the Bible.

Reflecting and Recording

Go back to your reflection today about your thoughts and feelings of the past week or two and the pattern of recurring thoughts and dreams. Read your notes, then in the space below Psalm 138 (on page 55), write your prayer, guided by the thoughts of the psalmist but with the content of your thoughts and feelings recorded and offered to God for clarity and healing.

Day Six: *Intercession and Petition*

As mentioned on the first day of this week, prayer is so expansive in its range of expression, so pivotal to our spiritual growth, so mysterious, rich, and intimately personal, that its depths can never be plumbed. Thus the necessity for discipline. We keep growing in our understanding, and we continue to explore ways of praying.

Even in a week's emphasis on this particular discipline for spiritual growth, we must at least look briefly at *intercession*. The Christian who prays turns inevitably to prayer for others. Let's look at a story of intercession and healing in the New Testament.

> Jesus went away from there and withdrew to the district of Tyre and Sidon. And behold, a Canaanite woman from that region came out and cried, "Have mercy on me, O Lord, Son of David; my daughter is severely possessed by a demon." But he did not answer her a word. And his disciples came and begged him, saying, "Send her away, for she is crying after us." He answered, "I was sent only to the lost sheep of the house of Israel." But she came and knelt before him, saying, "Lord, help me." And he answered, "It is not fair to take the children's bread and throw it to the dogs." She said, "Yes, Lord, yet even the dogs eat the crumbs that fall from their master's table." Then Jesus answered her, "O woman, great is your faith! Be it done for you as you desire." And her daughter was healed instantly.
>
> —Matthew 15: 21–28

There are some attention-getting moments in this story. At first Jesus refuses to answer the woman's plea: "He did not answer her a word.'' Prayer is now tested, and we can gain some helpful insight from what happens here.

Note that the woman is asking, as any of us would ask, for the healing of her daughter. She is right in this asking, and she comes in complete faith. She doesn't question whether Jesus *can* heal; she obviously believes ardently that he can. The need is there, the faith is present, the prayer is worthy, yet no response from Jesus.

At this point the disciples begged him to send her away. If the silence of Jesus to the woman's plea seems strange, what happens now is even stranger. Jesus addresses the disciples: ''I was sent only to the lost sheep of the house of Israel.'' You have to wonder whether Jesus is really speaking to the disciples or to the woman. And what he says is so out of character with his ministry. It can't be that he means the woman's request cannot be responded to because she is a Canaanite and not of the ''house of Israel.'' Can it?

Puzzled forever we may be by that but not by what happens next. Overhearing this word, the woman presses her request. ''I may be the wrong kind of person, a pagan not a Jew, but even dogs eat crumbs that fall from their master's table'' (AP). She appeals to the love of Jesus. Acknowledging no right to a loaf, she asks for crumbs. When Jesus sensed this faith in his love, he responded, and her daughter was healed.

Anthony Bloom has a marvelous comment on this story.

So often we implore God, saying, ''O God, if . . . if Thou wilt . . . if Thou canst . . . ,'' just like the father, who says to Christ: ''Your disciples have not been able to cure my little boy, if you can do anything, do it'' (Mk 9:22). Christ answers with another ''if'': if you believe, however little, everything is possible with faith. Then the man says: ''I believe, help thou mine unbelief.'' The two ''ifs'' are correlative, because if there is no faith there is also no possibility for God to enter into the situation. . . .

Whenever by faith the kingdom of God is re-created, there is a place for the laws of the kingdom to act, that is for God to come into the situation with his wisdom, his ability to do good within an evil situation, without, however, upsetting the whole world. Our ''if'' refers less to the power of God than to his love and concern; and God's reply ''if you can believe in my love, everything is possible'' means that no miracle can happen unless, even in an incipient way, the kingdom of God is present.

A miracle is not the breaking of the laws of the fallen world, it is the re-establishment of the laws of the kingdom of God; a miracle happens only if we believe that the law depends not on the power but on the love of God although we know that God is almighty, as long as we think that he does not care, no miracle is possible; to work it God would have to enforce his will, and that he does not do, because at the very core of his relationship to the world, even fallen, there is his absolute respect for human freedom and rights. The moment you say: "I believe, and that is why I turned to you," implies: "I believe that you will be willing, that there is love in you, that you are actually concerned about every single situation." The moment this grain of faith is there the right relationship is established and a miracle becomes possible (Bloom, pp. 70–72).

So here is a signal clue for our intercession. We begin by believing in the love of God as we see it in Jesus Christ. We then willingly trust God to act powerfully in love.

So we can link our intercession with the practice of contemplative prayer as recognizing, cultivating awareness, and giving expression to the indwelling Christ (Day Two of this week). We bring those for whom we are concerned into our awareness of the indwelling Christ, thus we bring them to Christ. I doubt if there is a more powerful way of praying for another than to simply hold in our awareness a vision of the person for whom we are praying along with a vision of the loving Christ healing and tending to the needs of others.

Reflecting and Recording

Spend some time thinking about the matter of trusting *first* God's love, rather than God's power. Do you have difficulty trusting that love or believing in that power? Make some notes here.

Spend some time now praying in this fashion for two or three persons about whom you are concerned. Get a vision of Jesus healing—think of the woman with the issue of blood touching the hem of his garment (Mark 5:25–34) or the man living among the tombs (Mark 5:1–13) or the blind man crying out from the crowd (Mark 10:46–52). Now live in that awareness of the healing Christ, and bring those for whom you would pray to Christ in your own awareness.

Day Seven: *The Legitimate "If"*

It is hard to find legitimacy in doubting that God loves us because the witness of scripture is so clear. If we had only the cross, that should be enough to forever convince us that God loves unconditionally, unendingly, and at terrific cost. However, as Anthony Bloom has reminded us, there is a legitimate "if" for our praying.

> We can say: "I am asking this, if it is according to thy will, or if it is for the best, or if there is no secret evil intention in me when I ask," and so on. All these "ifs" are more than legitimate, because they imply a diffident attitude to our own selves; and every prayer of petition should be an "if-prayer" . . . In the majority of cases we do not know what Christ would have prayed for in this situation and so we introduce the "if", which means that as far as we can see, as far as we know God's will, this is what we wish to happen to meet his will. But the "if" also means; I am putting into these words my desire that the best should happen, and therefore you can alter this concrete petition to anything you choose, taking my intention, the desire that your will be done, even if I am unwise in stating how I should like it to be done (Bloom, pp. 72–73).

Again, with this legitimate "if" incorporated in our prayer, we can link intercession with our contemplative style of praying—recognizing, cultivating awareness of, and giving expression to the indwelling Christ. This is what Paul teaches us.

> I consider that the sufferings of this present time are not worth comparing with the glory that is to be revealed to us. For the creation waits with eager longing for the revealing of the sons of God; for the creation was subjected to futility, not of its own will but by the will of him who subjected it in hope; because the creation itself will be set free from its bondage to decay and obtain the glorious liberty of the children of God. We know that the whole creation has been groaning in travail together until now; and not only the creation, but we ourselves, who have the first fruits of the Spirit, groan inwardly as we wait for adoption as sons, the redemption of our bodies. For in this hope we were saved. Now hope that is seen is not hope. For who hopes for what he sees? But if we hope for what we do not see, we wait for it with patience.
>   Likewise the Spirit helps us in our weakness; for we do not know how to pray as we ought, but the Spirit himself intercedes for us with sighs too deep for words. And he who searches the hearts of men knows that is the mind of the Spirit, because the Spirit intercedes for the saints according to the will of God
>   —Romans 8:18–27

Often we do not know the needs of those for whom we wish to pray. We can't even find words to express our feelings. We are silent, but our concern is deep. We groan within. In that spirit, we deliberately get a vision of the loving, caring, healing Christ, and we bring into that awareness those for whom we would pray, placing them and the whole situation in his care.

An aspect of this prayer of Christ awareness must always be giving expression to the indwelling Christ. At the heart of prayer is commitment—commitment of ourselves to Christ, commitment of those persons and situations for which we pray to Christ, and commitment of ourselves to be expressions of Christ as an answer to our praying.

Reflecting and Recording

Again let's pray by recognizing and cultivating awareness of the indwelling Christ. Get a vision of Jesus healing the woman who touched the hem of his garment (Mark 5:25–34). Also visualize him forgiving the woman taken in the act of adultery, about to be stoned, but forgiven by Jesus (John 8:1–11). Picture him, too, caring for the daily needs of people, feeding the five thousand (John 6:1–14). Alive in your awareness of Christ, bring into the awareness those for whom you would pray. Simply stay alive in the awareness of these persons being ministered to by Christ.

Now, focus on your awareness of Christ and your relationship to these persons for whom you are praying and their need. Is there something Christ would do for these persons that you may actually do as his presence to them? With that question, listen to Christ as you look at those for whom you are praying.

Write here what you have heard and what you are going to do as an act of commitment.

Group Meeting for Week Two

Introduction

Participation in a group such as this is a covenant relationship. You will profit most as you keep the daily discipline of the thirty-minute period and as you faithfully attend these weekly meetings. Do not feel guilty if you have to miss a day in the workbook or be discouraged if you are not able to give the full thirty minutes in daily discipline. Don't hesitate sharing that with the group. We may learn something about ourselves as we share. We may discover, for instance, that we are unconsciously afraid of looking seriously at these disciplines because of what may be required of us. Be patient with yourself and always be open to what God may be seeking to teach you.

Our growth in part hinges upon our group participation, so share as openly and honestly as you can. Listen to what persons are saying. Sometimes there is meaning beyond the surface of their words which you may pick up if you are really attentive.

Being a sensitive participant in this fashion is crucial. Responding immediately to the feelings we pick up is also crucial. Sometimes it is important for the group to focus its entire attention upon a particular individual. If some need or concern is expressed, it may be appropriate for the leader to ask the group to enter into a brief period of special prayer for the persons or concerns revealed. Participants should not always depend upon the leader for this kind of sensitivity, for the leader may miss it. Even if you aren't the leader, don't hesitate to ask the group to join you in special prayer. This praying may be silent, or some person may wish to lead the group in prayer.

Remember, you have a contribution to make to the group. What you consider trivial or unimportant may be just what another person needs to hear. We are not seeking to be profound but simply to share our experience.

Sharing Together

Note: It will not be possible in the time frame to use all these suggestions. The leader should select what will be most beneficial to the group. It is important that the leader be thoroughly familiar with these suggestions in order to move through them selectively according to the direction in which the group is moving.

1. Begin your time together with the entire group reading in

unison the psalm selections printed in Day One of this week. Follow this by singing the well-known doxology by Thomas Ken:

> Praise God, from whom all blessings flow;
> Praise him, all creatures here below;
> Praise him above, ye heavenly host;
> Praise Father, Son, and Holy Ghost. Amen.

2. Let each person share the most meaningful day in this week's workbook adventure.

3. Now share the most difficult day and tell why it was difficult.

4. On Day One of this week you were asked to recall a time when you were aware of being known and loved by God. Invite two or three persons to share their experiences, no one taking more than three minutes to do so.

5. Also on Day One, you were asked to get in touch with an experience when you felt separated, not known, not loved by God. Invite two or three people to share their experiences, taking no more than three minutes for each to do so.

6. Let the group reflect on these two sets of experiences in comparison. Compare the circumstances surrounding the experiences. Were the persons living a disciplined life of prayer at the time? Were they involved in worship and Christian fellowship? What lessons are here?

7. Spend eight or ten minutes with the group talking about prayer as "recognizing, cultivating awareness of, and giving expression to the indwelling Christ" (Day Two). Is this a new concept? Have you sensed it before but never quite focused on it in that fashion? Has your praying in the past given expression to that idea?

8. What sort of experience did you have with Day Six—practicing intercession by bringing the person about whom you are concerned into your awareness of the indwelling Christ? Do you think this style of praying may enhance your practice of intercession?

Praying Together

As stated last week, the effectiveness of this group and the quality of relationship will be enhanced by a commitment to praying for each other by name each day. If a polaroid camera is available, following the session tonight take a picture of each person in the group. Put these pictures face down on a table and let each person "draw" a picture. This person will be the focus of special prayer for the week. Bring the photos back next week, shuffle them and draw again. Continue this throughout your pilgrimage together. Looking at a person's picture as you pray for that person will add meaning. Having the picture will also remind you that you are to give special prayer attention to this person during the week.

1. Praying corporately each week is a special ministry. Take some time now for a period of verbal prayer, allowing each person to mention any special needs he or she wishes to share with the entire group.

A good pattern is to ask for a period of prayer after each need is mentioned. There may be silent prayer by the entire group, or someone may offer a brief two-or-three-sentence verbal prayer.

2. Close your time by praying together the great prayer of the church, "Our Father." As you pray this prayer, remember that you are linking yourselves with all Christians of all time in universal intercession.

Words of Encouragement

As you begin this third week of your journey, here are some thoughts to keep in mind:

Discipline is an important dimension of life. Discipline is not slavish rigidity but an ordering of life that enables you to control your circumstances rather than controlled by them. For most people, a designated time of prayer is essential for building a.life of prayer.

If you have not yet established a regular time to use this workbook and as your "prayer time," try to find the right time for you this week. Experiment: in the morning, after work, during the lunch hour, before retiring. Find time that seems best for you.

If you discover that you can't cover all the workbook material and exercises given for a day, don't berate yourself. Get what you can out of what you do. There is no point in rushing over three or four steps or principles if you cannot think deeply. Pray seriously about them one by one.

Intellectual assent to a great principle or possibility is important, but it does us little good until we act upon it—until we say yes in our minds.

Don't hesitate to make decisions and resolves, but don't condemn yourself if you fail. God is patient and wants us to be patient with ourselves.

Confession

Day One: *The Primary Need for Confession*

The primary need for confession is simple: that we might experience forgiveness.

The witness of the scripture is that the dominant desire in God's heart is the desire to forgive. David must have known this, so he prayed.

> Have mercy on me, O God,
>   according to thy steadfast love;
> according to thy abundant mercy
>   blot out my transgressions.
> Wash me thoroughly from my iniquity,
>   and cleanse me from my sin!
>
> For I know my transgressions,
>   and my sin is ever before me.
> Against thee, thee only, have I sinned,
>   and done that which is evil in thy sight,
> so that thou art justified in thy sentence
>   and blameless in thy judgment.
> Behold, I was brought forth in iniquity,
>   and in sin did my mother conceive me.
>
> Behold, thou desirest truth in the inward being;
>   therefore teach me wisdom in my secret heart.
> Purge me with hyssop, and I shall be clean;
>   wash me, and I shall be whiter than snow.

Fill me with joy and gladness;
let the bones which thou hast broken rejoice.
Hide thy face from my sins,
And blot out all my iniquities.

Create in me a clean heart, O God,
and put a new and right spirit within me.
Cast me not away from thy presence,
and take not thy holy Spirit from me.
Restore to me the joy of thy salvation,
and uphold me with a willing spirit.
—Psalm 51:1–12

It is also clear in the New Testament that the dominant desire of God's heart is to forgive. The story of the woman caught in the act of adultery is a vivid witness. When the accusing men bring the woman to Jesus, it puts Jesus in a "no-win" dilemma. If he elects to show mercy on the woman and free her, he will clearly be disobeying Jewish law; if he condemns her or does not intervene in preventing condemnation, he will be going against everything he has taught about compassion and forgiveness.

The problem is clear—sin and the need for forgiveness. Jesus expands the focus. He does not deal only with the sin of the woman; he forces the accusers to look at themselves. In both instances—the adulteress and her accusers—confession and forgiveness is Jesus' aim. Look closely at Jesus' action.

The accusers make their charge, but they are not prepared for Jesus' response. They must have been speechless, immobilized by Jesus' offer, "Let him who is without sin among you be the first to throw a stone at her" (John 8:7). Jesus then bends over to write in the sand. Was he allowing the people some relief from their own engagement with him in order that they might deal with their own consciences? Or did he write something that probed even more deeply and burned more searingly upon their calloused hearts? Whatever, when he arose there was no one present to condemn the woman, and Jesus announced to her his forgiveness and call to a new life.

In her book *Learning to Forgive,* Doris Donnelly offers a perceptive commentary on this action of Jesus. She says that he bound "the accusers to their sins to render them capable of repentance. On the other hand, he offers to free the accused woman from the weight of her shame and guilt by forgiving her sin" (Donnelly, p. 114).

See how that confirms the witness of scripture: God's dominant desire to forgive. For the adulteress and for the accusers, Jesus was offering an opportunity for confession and forgiveness. We could add witness after witness from scripture. Beginning at the point of believing it is God's desire to forgive, confession becomes not a morbid discipline, not a dark, groveling in the mud and mire of life, not a fearful response to a wrathful, angry God who is out to get us if we don't shape up. Rather, confession becomes an act of anticipation, a response to the unconditional call of God's love: the promise that "the blood of Jesus his Son cleanses us from all sin" (1 John 1:7).

"The blood of Jesus . . . cleanses us." Here we come to the meaning of the cross. Our redemption by Jesus on the cross is a great mystery hidden in the heart of God. To try to reduce it to a formula or to work out a rational system of courts and judges and payments of penalties or priests and sacrifices of appeasement is to try to bring it down to a human level and always to miss a measure of its power. The effective redemptive power of the cross is not in our understanding.

It is necessary to note two truths as the cross is related to confession and forgiveness. One, the cross is the expression of God's great desire to forgive. Not anger, but love brought Jesus to the cross. Two, without the cross and the forgiveness which is the core of its meaning, confession is merely psychologically therapeutic.

Reflecting and Recording

Live for a few minutes with the affirmation that love, not anger, brought Jesus to the cross, and that the cross is the expression of God's great desire to forgive. Ponder the meaning of that and write a prayer of thanksgiving in response to this fact.

Day Two: *Self-Examination and Confession*

If we claim to be sinless, we are self-deceived and strangers to the truth. If we confess our sins, he is just, and may be trusted to forgive our sins and cleanse us from every kind of wrong; but if we say we have committed no sin, we make him out to be a liar, and then his word has no place in us.

—1 John 1:8–10, NEB

Self-examination and confession go together as one discipline. One of the primary purposes of this discipline is to keep us aware of our true condition. We are masters of the art of self-deceit. In many instances others see us better than we see ourselves.

One of the greatest barriers to personal wholeness and spiritual growth and maturity is our becoming unaware of, or unconscious of, our sin and guilt. John was right, "If we claim to be sinless, we are self-deceived and strangers to the truth." The Revised Standard Version of First John 1:8 is even stronger: "If we say we have no sin, we deceive ourselves, *and the truth is not in us*" (italics added).

What happens is rather clear. We know that there is a tension between good and evil within us, but we are fearful of dealing with that tension. We suppress our feelings. We begin to suppress the conflicts between our warring passions. When a sinful lust or desire emerges we push it under the rug of our consciousness. We do this so much that we lose track of the truth and to some degree numb ourselves to the conflict.

Behind our fear of dealing with the tension between good and evil within us is the false notion that to admit sin is to admit weakness and failure, to risk being accepted by others and even by God. I can understand how that may be so in relation to others. But just how this has come about in relation to God is a mystery. The heart of the gospel is the graceful forgiveness of a loving God. And, in fact, the essential for forgiveness and healing is *confession*. "If we confess our sins, he [Jesus Christ] is just, and may be trusted to forgive our sins and cleanse us from every kind of wrong."

Yesterday we noted two meanings of the cross as related to confession. One, the cross is the expression of God's great desire to forgive. Two, without the cross, confession is only psychologically therapeutic. There is positive value of confession simply at the level of psychological therapy, but our focus is greater than that. We are working with discipline for spiritual growth.

One of history's most inspiring biographies of spiritual growth is that of Brother Lawrence. He lived in seventeenth-century France and found his growth in Christian maturity as a dishwasher in a monastery through what he calls "The Practice of the Presence of God." This is one of the ways he tells of his growth:

> I have no pain or difficulty about my state, because I have no will but that of God, which I endeavor to accomplish in all things, and to which I am so resigned that I would not take up a straw from the ground against his order, or for any other motive than purely that of love to him. . . .
>
> I think it proper to inform you after what manner I consider myself before God. . . .

I consider myself as the most wretched of men [that is, imperfect and faulty], full of sores and corruption, and who has committed all sorts of crimes against his King [that is, against his real self as God, the King, sees it]. Touched with a sensible regret, I confess to him all my wickedness [it is wicked to keep an impossible goal and fail of the good and beautiful which is my potential], I ask this forgiveness, I abandon myself in his hands that he may do what he pleases with me. The King, full of mercy and goodness, very far from chastising me, embraces me with love, makes me eat at his table, serves me with his own hands, gives me the keys of his treasures;...in a thousand and a thousand ways, [he blesses me] (Lawrence, p. 24, 25–26).

All of this was the result of honest confession, in light of the cross, to God whose dominant desire is to forgive. Brother Lawrence knew himself forgiven and accepted in the love of God.

In his work he continued his familiar conversation with his Maker, . . . offering to him all his actions. . . . When he had finished he examined himself how he had discharged his duty; if he found well, he returned thanks to God; if otherwise, he asked pardon, and without being discouraged, he set his mind right again, and continued his exercise of the presence of God, as if he had never deviated from it. "Thus," said he, "by rising after my falls, and by frequently renewed acts of faith and love, I am come to a state wherein it would be as difficult for me not to think of God as it was at first to accustom myself to it" (Lawrence, p. 19).

When we practice confession in the fashion of Brother Lawrence, with the love of God expressed in the cross as the dynamic invitation to which we are responding, our relationship to God changes. We do not remain separated, estranged, under judgment; we are accepted. This is an objective change in our relationship to God. There is also a subjective change, a change in us. We are no longer paralyzed with guilt. We no longer feel mean or ugly or dirty or powerless or sick of heart and mind. We are healed. We experience an inner transformation.

Reflecting and Recording

In the next few days we will look at some specific guides for self-examination and confession. Let's begin today with one simple exercise. Imagine that you and I are alone together. We have been having a conversation about our Christian life and growth. I say to you, "_____, I really believe that you are unaware of the tension between good and evil in your life. I don't believe that you are acknowledging the power of sin within you."

Think about that. Is it true? How is it true? To what degree is it true? How would you respond to me? Write your response.

We connect self-examination and confession as one discipline because they are one. I doubt if there can ever be a *complete* confession. There is too much about us that is hidden; stirrings, even evil stirrings deep within are suppressed so solidly that we may never come to complete self-knowledge. An ongoing discipline of self-examination and confession is essential.

Look at our model, Brother Lawrence. "When he had finished he examined himself how he had discharged his duty; if he found well, he returned thanks to God; if otherwise, he asked pardon, and without being discouraged, he set his mind right again, and continued his exercise of the presence of God, as if he had never deviated from it" (Lawrence, p. 19). Once we have confessed, we leave our sins and failures behind, seeking to live as though we had never separated ourselves from God by our sin.

Make whatever confession you feel you need to make now, and go from this time and place confident of the loving presence of God.

Day Three: *The Problem of Pride*

William Sloane Coffin was the chaplain at Yale University for many years and is now the pastor of Riverside Church in New York City, probably America's most famous church. In his autobiography, *Once to Every Man,* he tells of having gone through a divorce. Shortly after this painful experience, he was with his good friend Abraham Heschel, a Jewish rabbi and one of the great philosophers of our time. They were walking along a street in New York toward the rabbi's apartment, when Heschel turned to Coffin and said:

> "I understand, my friend, that you have been through some suffering."
>
> "That's right, Father Abraham, it's been hell. It still is."
>
> "You should have called me," he said.
>
> "You were in Los Angeles all summer."
>
> "You still could have called me."
>
> "Well, I didn't want to bother you. Besides, I had other friends I could talk to and I don't like talking about such things over the phone."
>
> "That was a mistake. I could have helped you."
>
> Irked by his self-assurance I stopped and faced him. "All right, how could you have helped me?"
>
> As I had seen him do so often he raised his shoulders and his hands, palms up. "I would have told you about my father, the great Hasidic rabbi, blessed be his memory, who too was divorced. You see, you Christians are so vexed by your perfectionism. It is always your undoing."
>
> He continued to talk in this vein, and I felt the tears starting down my cheeks. He was so right. And it was nice that a Jew was reminding a Christian that his salvation lay not in being sinless, but in accepting his forgiveness. Without pausing, he wiped my face with his handkerchief. Then after again assuring me that God still loved me—"even as I do, and maybe more"—he said, "Now we shall continue to my apartment" (Coffin, pp. 289–290).

What is it that keeps us from confessing? Is it pride? Do we know that confession is a means of healing, for healing is not in being perfect but in being forgiven? Look at some scripture:

> Two men went up into the temple to pray, one a Pharisee and the other a tax collector. The Pharisee stood and prayed thus with himself, "God, I thank thee that I am not like other men, extortioners, unjust, adulterers, or even like this tax collector. I fast twice a week, I give tithes of all that I get." But the tax collector, standing far off, would not even lift up his eyes to heaven, but beat his breast, saying, "God, be merciful to me a

sinner!'' I tell you, this man went down to his house justified rather than the other; for every one who exalts himself will be humbled, but he who humbles himself will be exalted.

—Luke 18:10–14

There are three obvious lessons in this story of Jesus:

One, the Pharisee prayed *with* himself. ''The Pharisee stood and prayed thus with himself.'' There was no confession here. The Pharisee was not praying but informing God how good he was.

Two, no person who is proud can remain proud and pray. Pride and self-righteousness are sure barriers separating us from God. A man asked an old rabbi, ''How come God appeared to men in olden days but nobody sees him today?'' ''Because today,'' the rabbi responded, ''no one can bow low enough.''

Three, honesty about ourselves comes not from comparing ourselves to others but by putting ourselves in the presence of God, seeing ourselves in the light of his holiness and love. The Pharisee, no doubt, did what he said he did, but he had the wrong point of comparison: ''I thank thee that I am not like other men.''

William Barclay tells of traveling by train from Scotland to England. As the train passed through the Yorkshire moors he saw a little whitewashed cottage. It fairly glimmered in radiant whiteness. Some days later Barclay made the return journey to Scotland. Snow had fallen, completely blanketing the ground. Coming again to the little white cottage, Barclay was surprised to see that what had appeared shimmering white, now seemed drab and soiled and almost grey in comparison to the virgin whiteness of the new fallen snow.

In Jesus' story, the Pharisee was comparing himself to others; the tax collector was looking at his life in relation to God.

Reflecting and Recording

Saint Francis of Assisi said that what a person is in the sight of God so much he is and no more. We do not get to the depth of healing, cleansing confession until we begin to sense what we are in God's sight. Begin to practice that now. The two columns below will give you a guide and structure for this. First focus on action, then on attitudes and feelings. God not only knows what you do, but what you think and feel as well. Also, God sees the positive as well as the negative. We need to stay aware that confession means naming ourselves as we are before God, the positive and the negative.

So first, deal with your *actions*. Begin with today and keep pushing back into the past week. Record the big and the little events, relationships, actions, experiences which come to your mind, putting them in the positive and negative columns as you think God would perceive them in you. Then move to attitudes.

Actions
Positive   *Negative*

Attitudes and Feelings
Positive   *Negative*

Of course God sees us as we are, and God sees us more clearly and completely than we see ourselves. One of the purposes of confession is to practice seeing ourselves as God sees us. To discipline ourselves in this fashion strikes a telling blow to our pride and opens us to receive God's grace. We begin to realize that God's love is not dependent upon our performance. God loves us, *period*. The more aware we are of God's loving acceptance, the more our actions will be in harmony with God's will.

The first lesson we noted from the story of the praying of the Pharisee and the tax collector was the Pharisee's prayer *with himself*. As you pray now, to close this period, be careful that you talk with God, not with yourself.

Day Four: *Examination of Conscience*

As already indicated, self-examination and confession go together. In self-examination and confession we clarify our vision and understanding of who we are before God and in relation to others. Paul said, "Examine yourselves, to see whether you are holding to your faith" (2 Cor. 13:5). To be a discipline for spiritual growth confession must be grounded in two realities.

One, confession is essential because our sins separate us from God. Isaiah said, "Your iniquities have made a separation between you and your God, and your sins have hid his face from you so that he does not hear" (Isa. 59:2).

The second reality, which is the antidote for the first, is that sin does not have to separate us from God. John said, "If we confess our sins, he is faithful and just, and will forgive our sins and cleanse us from all unrighteousness" (1 John 1:9).

So the dynamics of self-examination and confession are at the heart of an open, growing relationship with God. A deliberate expression of this discipline is what we may call *examination of conscience*. As a daily discipline, we may set a specific time. I find it most effective in the evening, just before I go to sleep. I replay the day, moving through it hour by hour in my mind—from situation to situation, job to job, relationship to relationship. Did I do my best in that job? Was I understanding and kind in that relationship? Did I speak the truth in love? Was I condemning? Judgmental? Did I fail to speak when I should have? Did I allow someone to hurt another by idle gossip without raising a question? Did I write the needed letter or make the helpful telephone call or visit? Was I lustful? Covetous? Jealous? Callous? Did I fail to witness for Christ in any available opportunity?

There is a need for a periodic examination of conscience, not daily but more appropriately weekly, as it relates to our *ministry*. One effective way of doing this is to recall Jesus' parable of the last judgment in Matthew 25:31–46. We may set aside one of our daily examinations of conscience for this focus or choose some other specific time. The service of holy communion is especially appropriate for this. As I await my turn to go to the Lord's table to receive the bread and wine, I find it a challenge to examine myself to see if I am holding to my faith (2 Cor. 13:5).

In this examination of conscience, we ask ourselves if we did it "to the least of these." We rehearse Jesus' words, "I was hungry and you gave me food, I was thirsty and you gave me drink . . . I was naked and you clothed me, I was sick and you visited me . . . in prison and you came to me" (Matt. 25:35–36). *Did we?*

We need to make a *literal* response to these calls of Jesus. We also need to examine ourselves in a more encompassing way. Cries come from persons who are hungry and thirsty for spiritual food and moral support. There are persons who are well fed and sheltered but need to be clothed in friendship. There are persons locked in prisons of destructive habits, demeaning jobs, painful relationships, who need our love and support.

Reflecting and Recording

Look back over the past twenty-four hours. Move through this period hour by hour, from situation to situation, job to job, relationship to relationship, using the suggestion given previously for a daily examination of conscience (not examination of conscience in relation to ministry). Make notes here about your sins and failures. Be as specific as possible.

Did this deliberate process assist you in sharpening your confession? The more specific we are in our confession, the less likely we are to fall into the tempting snare of covering up and suppressing. The more open we are with ourselves and God the healthier we are spiritually. This openness enhances the possibility for growth.

Practice this daily examination of conscience before you sleep tonight to see if closing the day in this fashion is meaningful to you. If you are serious about discipline for spiritual growth, practice this examination of conscience daily for at least a two-week period. Close each examination of conscience and confession by claiming John's promise: "If we confess our sins, he is faithful and just, and will forgive our sins and cleanse us from all unrighteousness" (1 John 1:9).

Day Five: *Naming the Demon*

Yesterday, we looked at a guide for examination of conscience focused on *ministry* and suggested that we engage in such a practice on a weekly basis. Go back and read the description of using Jesus' parable of the last judgment (Matt. 25:31–46) as the basis for self-examination. Do that now, then come back here for a suggested exercise.

Look now, in memory, at the past three days of your life and examine yourself in response to Jesus' call. Make some notes about your performance—not only your failures but your faithful responses to "the least of these."

Let's look now at confession as a process of *naming the demon*. When we examine ourselves and confess, we need to be explicit and *name* our failure, our sin, our problem, our guilt, our pain, our broken relationship, our poisoned attitude, our rampant passion—name these *specifically*. There is healing and redemptive power inherent in the naming process. Rollo May has written clearly and helpfully about this dynamic.

In the naming of the daimonic, there is an obvious and interesting parallel to the power of naming in contemporary medical and psychological therapy. At some time, everyone must have been aware of how relieved he was when he went to the doctor with a troublesome illness and the doctor pronounced a *name* for it. A name for the virus or germ, a name for the disease process, and the doctor could then make a statement or two about the disease on the basis of this name.

Now something deeper is going on in this phenomenon than our relief at whether or not the doctor can predict a quick cure. Or any cure, for that matter. Some years ago, after weeks of undetermined illness, I heard from a specialist that my sickness was tuberculosis. I was, I recall, distinctly relieved, *even though I was fully aware that this meant, in those days, that medicine could do nothing to cure the disease*. A number of explanations will leap to the reader's mind. He will accuse me of being glad to be relieved from responsibility; that any patient is reassured when he has the authority of the doctor to which he can give himself up; and the naming of the disorder takes away the mystery of it. But these explanations are surely too simple. Even the last one—that the naming reduces the mystery—will be seen, on further thought, as an illusion: to me the bacillus or the virus or the germ is still as much a mystery as ever, and the tubular bacillus was then still a mystery to the doctor.

The relief, rather, comes from the *act of confronting the daimonic world of illness by means of the names*. The doctor and I stand together, he knowing more names in this purgatory than I and therefore technically my guide into hell. Diagnosis (from *dia-gignoskein*, literally "knowing through") may be thought of, on one side, as our modern form of calling the name of the offending demon. Not that the rational information about the disease is unimportant; but the rational data given to me add up to something more significant than the information itself. It becomes, for me, a symbol of a change to a new way of life. The names are symbols of a certain attitude I must take toward this daimonic situation of illness; the disorder expresses a myth (a total pattern of life) which communicates to me a way in which I must now orient and order my life. This is so whether it is for two weeks with a cold or twelve years with tuberculosis; the *quantity* of time is not the point. It is the quality of life (May, pp. 172–173).

Reflecting and Recording

May says, naming becomes "a symbol of a change to a new way of life. The names are symbols of a certain attitude I must take toward this daimonic situation of illness." Let's reflect upon this in an expanded sense.

A personal witness. At a particular period, I went through an anguishing time in relation to my son. All sorts of confused and complex ingredients were operative. I felt impatient in the relationship, unable to keep any sort of clear perspective. My responses and reactions to him were anything but consistent. My temper fuse became shorter and shorter, my perception blurred, and I found myself often trying desperately to escape dealing with the issue. A counselor-friend helped me clarify perceptions and keep perspective. But my greatest help came when I began to "name the demon." In fact there was more than one demon.

I realized that I was an *indulgent* parent. I was a "softie" and easily "conned." The measure and style of discipline had not worked the same with my three children. I went through periods of self-condemnation, feeling the devastating guilt of failure. Naming all that enabled me to cope, but my greatest freedom came when I named the big demon which was fear. It was a fear for my son's future, but it was a fear tied with my own life struggle. I wanted him to have more options than I felt I had had. Naming that demon enabled me to deal with my own sense of achievement, but it also gave me a focus around which I could deal more objectively with the issues and more acceptingly with Kevin as a person.

Look at your own life now. Focus on some difficult relationship, some moral struggle, some addiction, some habit that is getting out of control, some "situation" that is really bugging you. What is really the core issue? Try to discover the demon. Name the demon by describing the situation as clearly as you can as I have tried to do in my above confession. Write that confession here.

You have already been praying as you have sought to name the demon or demons in your life. Continue your praying by asking God to assist you in keeping your demons in the open, not letting them hide; to give you perspective, wisdom, and strength to deal with your demons.

Day Six: *Locating Ourselves before God*

And he came out and went, as was his custom, to the Mount of Olives; and the disciples followed him. And when he came to the place he said to them, "Pray that you may not enter into temptation." And he withdrew from them about a stone's throw, and knelt down and prayed, "Father, if thou art willing, remove this cup from me; nevertheless not my will, but thine, be done." And when he rose from prayer, he came to the disciples and found them sleeping for sorrow, and he said to them, "Why do you sleep? Rise and pray that you may not enter into temptation."
                                                      —Luke 22: 39–46

Confession means more than recognizing and verbalizing our sins and failures, though that is an essential part of it. It means locating ourselves before God, honestly sharing who we are—our feelings and longings, our fears and frustrations, our hopes and dreams, our failures and triumphs. The honest sharing of who we are is always essential for authentic relationship. Confession means locating ourselves honestly before God.

Here is a clear example of it out of the life of Martin Luther King, Jr. One night in the middle of the tension of the Montgomery bus boycott, Dr. King was awakened by the phone. An angry voice said, "Listen, nigger, we've taken all we want from you. Before next week you'll be sorry you ever came to Montgomery." His caller hung up, but King couldn't sleep. Fear gripped him in its steel vice. Listen to his testimony:

I got out of bed and began to walk the floor. Finally, I went to the kitchen and heated a pot of coffee. I was ready to give up. I tried to think of a way to move out of the picture without appearing to be a coward. In this state of exhaustion, when my courage had almost gone, I determined to take my problem to God. My head in my hands, I bowed over the kitchen table and prayed aloud. The words I spoke to God that midnight are still vivid in my memory. "I am here taking a stand for what I believe is right. But now I am afraid. The people are looking to me for leadership, and if I stand before them without strength and courage, they too will falter. I am at the end of my powers. I have nothing left. I've come to the point where I can't face it alone" (King, p. 113).

King located himself honestly before God. This is absolutely essential for our relationship with God to be vital. Jesus demonstrated this pattern: "My God, my God, why hast thou forsaken me?"(Matt. 27:46); "Father, into thy hands I commend my spirit" (Luke 23:46, KJV).

It is only when we have thus located ourselves in this fashion that we are open to hearing and receiving from God what he wishes to offer. I didn't finish King's testimony earlier. After he named himself before God, God named him. This was King's confession:

At that moment, I experienced the presence of the Divine as I had never before experienced him. It seemed as though I could hear the quiet assurance of an inner voice, saying, "Stand up for righteousness, stand up for truth. God will be at your side forever." Almost at once my fears began to pass from me. My uncertainty disappeared. I was ready to face anything (King, p. 113).

Again, though, we must stay aware of the fact that confession as locating of ourselves before God is not always a confession of sin or a cry of need. It may be an expression of joy, a shout of praise, an exclamation of surprise and gratitude for being graced by some relationship, some gift.

Sarah and Abraham are witnesses of this honest response to God and to life. When God told Abraham that Sarah was going to have a child, he "fell on his face and laughed" (Gen. 17:17); likewise Sarah, when the news came to her (Gen. 18:12). Frederick Buechner comments on their behavior:

Why did the two old crocks laugh? They laughed because they knew only a fool would believe that a woman with one foot in the grave was soon going to have her other foot in the maternity ward. They laughed because God expected them to believe it anyway. They laughed because God seemed to believe it. They laughed because they half-believed it themselves. They laughed because laughing felt better than crying. They laughed because if by some crazy chance it just happened to come true they would really have something to laugh about, and in the meanwhile it helped keep them going (Buechner, p. 25).

Reflecting and Recording

Confession is locating ourselves before God. Yesterday, you sought to discover, name, and describe a "demon" in your life. Today, let's not restrict your confession to the negative, to sin or demons—though you may still want to acknowledge consciously that aspect of your experience.

Locate yourself before God by recognizing your *giftedness*. How do you feel gifted? What joys are you experiencing? What exciting, meaningful relationship or interpersonal involvement have you recently known? Likewise, what occasion for Sarah-Abraham laughter awaits you today? Write freely enough to locate yourself honestly before the Lord.

Offer now a prayer of thanksgiving and commitment.

Day Seven: *Standing before God with the Mind in the Heart*

> But who can discern his errors?
>   Clear thou me from hidden faults.
> Keep back thy servant also from presumptuous sins;
>   let them not have dominion over me!
> Then I shall be blameless,
>   and innocent of great transgression.
>
> Let the words of my mouth and the meditation of my heart
>   be acceptable in thy sight,
>   O Lord, my rock and my redeemer.
>
> —Psalm 19:12–14

One of the greatest Orthodox teachers of prayer, Bishop Theophan the Recluse, described the aim of Christian prayer in this fashion: "The principal thing is to stand before God with the mind in the heart, and to go on standing before him unceasingly day and night until the end of life."

Along with other writers of the eastern Christian tradition, Theophan kept the biblical idea of the heart as the center of the personality. They call deep inner prayer *the prayer of the heart*. In their understanding and language, the heart is our center as persons—the seat of our joys and conflicts, our feeling and passion, as well as the place of the Spirit. Prayer, then, serves to unify and integrate our personality.

To pray is to stand before God "with the mind in the heart." That means we are to focus, to center our attention, to bring the thoughts and reflections of our mind to the core of our being, to our heart. We do not come to God with our feelings here, our thoughts there, our longings hither, and our fleshly and emotional passions yonder. We come as one, integrated, our total being drawn as steel to a magnet into the sphere of our heart—to our center where the Spirit meets us.

When we come to God in this fashion, confession is then translated into transformation. We have set the stage for change. Fritz Kunkel, in his book *In Search of Maturity,* makes the point clearly.

Expression of what we find within ourselves, honest and reckless expression before the face of the Eternal, assuming responsibility for what we are, even if we are unaware of it, and asking God to help us to master the wild horses, or to revive the skeletons of horses which we dig out during the long hours of our confessions—this is the psychological method of religious self-education. It is a way of bringing to consciousness our unconscious contents, and of establishing control over our hidden powers. It is the way to mature responsibility. It is the old way of the Psalmist: "Yet who can detect his lapses? Absolve me from my faults unknown! And hold thy servant back from wilful sins, from giving way to them'' (Psalm 19:12, 13, Moffatt).

Not in the presence of a minister or a psychologist, but in the presence of God, things change completely. If you hate your brother, and you pour out all your hatred, remembering at the same time, as much as you can, the presence of God—and your hatred does not change, then you are not sufficiently aware either of the presence of God or of your hatred, and probably of both. Be more honest, give vent to your emotions. You hate your brother: imagine his presence, before God tell him how you feel, kick him, scratch him. You are ten years old now—get up from your chair, don't pretend to be a wise old Buddha, pace the floor, yell, scream, punch the furniture, express yourself. Rant and rage until you are exhausted, or until you laugh at yourself (Kunkel, pp. 253–254).

Reflecting and Recording

Go back to Day Five and quickly review what you wrote in the ''Reflecting and Recording'' period—when you named the ''demon.'' In light of your thinking today, did you complete that work? Are there other demons you would name? Make some notes.

Now pray as you are led to pray.

Group Meeting for Week Three

Introduction

Two essential ingredients of a Christian fellowship are *feedback* and *follow-up*. Feedback is necessary to keep the group dynamic working positively for all participants. Follow-up is essential to express Christian concern and ministry.

The leader is primarily responsible for feedback in the group. All persons should be encouraged to share their feelings about how the group is functioning. Listening is crucial, but so is checking meaning in order that those who are sharing this pilgrimage may know that we really hear. We often mishear. "Are you saying ---------?" is a good check question. It takes only a couple of persons in a group, who listen and feedback in this fashion, to set the mood for the group.

Follow-up is the function of everyone. If we listen to what others are saying, we will discover needs and concerns beneath the surface, situations that deserve special prayer and attention. Make notes of these as the group shares. Follow up during the week with a telephone call, a written note of caring and encouragement, a visit. What distinguishes a Christian fellowship is caring in action. "My, how those Christians love one another!" So follow up each week with others in the group.

Sharing Together

It is important in a fellowship for persons to know each other, at least to some degree. In a Christian fellowship our "Christian" story is important.

1. Begin by inviting each person in the group to share his or her "story." The leader might say to the group, "Assume these friends do not know you. What has happened in your life as a Christian that you wish to share?" No person should take more than five minutes. The leader should be prepared to warn about time. After three minutes, note that the person has two more minutes to complete the story.

2. Spend four or five minutes now in thanksgiving prayer. Invite persons to offer brief sentence prayers expressing particular gratitude for the sharing.

3. Shift gears now. On Day Five, we considered the possibility of ''naming the demon'' as a healing, redemptive process. Invite as many as will to share their experiences in this area. Spend as much time with this as necessary, saving fifteen minutes for two more exercises before you close.

4. On Day Six, the emphasis was upon naming our giftedness and joy, as well as our demon. Talk about the relative ease and uneasiness in those two aspects of confession. Did anyone have a ''new kind'' of experience or come to a new understanding of confession with the emphasis on giftedness and joy as a part of confession? Share these.

5. Spend ten minutes now, if needed, allowing persons to raise questions or make comments about any other concerns about this week's pilgrimage.

Praying Together

1. The leader should take up the polaroid pictures of the group, shuffle them, and let each person draw a new one.

2. Invite each member of the group to spend two minutes in quiet prayer for the person whose picture he or she has drawn, focusing on what that person has shared in this meeting.

3. Close the time with sentence prayers, praying specifically about the needs shared in ''naming the demons.''

Week Four

Submission and Service

Day One: *Grounding Ourselves in Scripture*

The most difficult of all disciplines for spiritual growth is submission. Not only is it the most difficult, it is probably the most dangerous. When misunderstood and abused it can play havoc in our lives. Thus Richard Foster sounds a welcomed warning:

> Somehow the human species has an extraordinary knack for taking the best teaching and turning it to the worst ends. Nothing can put people into bondage like religion, and nothing in religion has done more to manipulate and destroy people than a deficient teaching on submission (Foster, p. 96).

Since submission is such a difficult discipline, with great potential for misunderstanding, confusion, and perverted expression, we need to clarify our own thinking. More than that we need to ground ourselves in scripture. So this first day of our focus on submission, let's immerse ourselves in scripture and play back against scripture our own present ideas and understanding.

First, to stimulate the expression of our own thinking and feeling about submission, do three things.

One: When you hear the word *submission,* what is the first thought or feeling that comes to your mind? Write it down in a sentence or just a series of words.

Two: Think for a moment about submission. Try to recover from memory a verse of scripture that comes to your mind in thinking about submission. Write that verse down in your own words as you recall it. You do not have to be exact.

Three: In no more than three sentences, write a definition of *submission*.

Before we go on, compare your definition of *submission* to what first came to your mind when you heard the word *submission* and to the scripture you connected with *submission*. Is your definition consistent with these first thoughts?

Now, let's go to scripture. The following verses come from a number of places in the New Testament. Read them slowly, don't skip one word or line.

> And he called to him the multitude with his disciples, and said to them, "If any man would come after me, let him deny himself and take up his cross and follow me. For whoever would save his life will lose it; and whoever loses his life for my sake and the gospel's will save it."
>
> —Mark 8:34–35

> But Jesus called them to him and said, "You know that the rulers of the Gentiles lord it over them, and their great men exercise authority over them. It shall not be so among you; but whoever would be great among you must be your servant, and whoever would be first among you must be your slave; even as the Son of man came not to be served but to serve, and to give his life as a ransom for many."
>
> —Matthew 20:25–28

For the love of Christ controls us, because we are convinced that one has died for all; therefore all have died. And he died for all, that those who live might live no longer for themselves but for him who for their sake died and was raised.

—2 Corinthians 5:14–15

Be kindly affectioned one to another with brotherly love; in honor preferring one another; not slothful in business; fervent in spirit; serving the Lord; rejoicing in hope; patient in tribulation; continuing instant in prayer; distributing to the necessity of saints; given to hospitality.

—Romans 12:10–13, KJV

But you are not to be called rabbi, for you have one teacher, and you are all brethren. And call no man your father on earth, for you have one Father, who is in heaven. Neither be called masters, for you have one master, the Christ. He who is greatest among you shall be your servant; whoever exalts himself will be humbled, and whoever humbles himself will be exalted.

—Matthew 23:8–12

Be subject to one another out of reverence for Christ.

—Ephesians 5:21

So if there is any encouragement in Christ, any incentive of love, any participation in the Spirit, any affection and sympathy, complete my joy by being of the same mind, having the same love, being in full accord and of one mind. Do nothing from selfishness or conceit, but in humility count others better than yourselves. Let each of you look not only to his own interests, but also to the interests of others.

—Philippians 2:1–4

This is not all the New Testament says about submission, but this is enough to go on. The above selections are consistent with the whole of the New Testament. So what is the primary focus? Try this. The New Testament teaching about submission deals primarily with the spirit with which we view, and in which we relate to and treat other people.

In the matter of submission as a spiritual discipline and as a principle of conduct, the New Testament is not concerned with a hierarchy of relationship but with a style of life that is grounded in mutual commitment of persons to each other. That commitment flows out of our commitment to Christ. Paul summed it up in Ephesians 5:21: "Be subject to one another out of reverence for Christ."

Reflecting and Recording

Now as a final act of reflection, in no more than three sentences define *submission* as you think Jesus or Paul would.

Pray now that you will have the "mind of Christ" in understanding and practicing submission.

Day Two: *Subject to One Another Out of Reverence to Christ*

In our week of emphasis upon scripture and devotional reading we proposed a way of studying scripture that involved four steps.
1. Underline key words.
2. What does this verse or passage say?
3. What does it say to me?
4. What action does this scripture call for?
Use just one part of that process now. Go back and reread the scripture we looked at yesterday. Read it slowly and underline the key words in each selection. When you have done so, copy those key words in the space provided here.

While the word *submission* is not a recurring one in your list, most of the key words call for concern for others. It is a special kind of concern that is willing to put the good of another above our own desires, even our own needs. "Do nothing from selfishness or conceit, but in humility count others better than yourselves. Let each of you look not to his own interests, but also to the interests of others" (Phil. 2:3–4).

The way of submission is a cross-way of life, and it is a call to all Christians not to a particular group. "Be subject to one another out of reverence for Christ" (Eph. 5:21) is the general principle by which all Christians are to be guided. We are commanded (all persons—men and women, parents and children, masters and slaves) to live a life of submission not because of our station in life, but because Jesus lived a life of submission and showed that such is the only way to find life.

> It is almost impossible for us to understand the radical nature of this teaching because we are so far removed from the world of Paul's day. In that day—and this persists in some cultures even now—persons were bound into a certain "station." The Greeks held that was the way the gods had created things; persons had no choice. This was especially true of women. Women were seen as chattel, things to be used at whim and fancy, without rights, little more than slaves.
>
> Those to whom first-century culture afforded no choice were addressed by Paul as *free;* they could decide. This was revolutionary. Why would he call wives, children, and slaves to submission? That was their lot already. But something had happened to them. The gospel had freed them from a subordinate station in society. Second-, third-, and fourth-class citizenship was challenged by the gospel, and those *condemned* to those classes knew it. Paul, then, is not calling for submission on the basis of the way things were, the station in which the gods had ordered matters. No New Testament writer did that. All contemporary customs of superordinate and subordinate were completely ignored. Everyone was "to count others better than themselves" (Phil. 2:3) and be subject to one another out of reverence for Christ.
>
> Wives were to be subject to their husbands not because that was a part of the natural order, but because submission is the style of all Christians. When wives and others began to live this way, the status quo was deprived of its divine sanction, of its inherent rightness and permanence, and a revolution of mutual respect, affirmation, and service began. As will presently be seen in Paul's admonition to husbands, there are no "high" or "low" positions in Christian marriage and home, nor in the entire Christian family. A new order has been born in which all participants regard themselves as servants of one Master, Jesus Christ, and give themselves in mutual service to one another because of him. (Dunnam, *The Communicator's Commentary,* Vol. 8, pp. 231–232).

Reflecting and Recording

An obvious place to begin the practice of submission is in the family. If we are not living in a traditional family setting, the most obvious focus would be our most intimate circle of friends. Select two persons in your family or two close friends. Name them beside numerals 1 and 2. In the space provided after each name make some notes about how you currently relate to that person. Are you submissive? How? In what ways might you express submission as a Christian discipline.

1. _____:

2. _____:

Spend some time reflecting upon your style of relating. Is submission a part of that style? In what way? How do you feel about submission? How might submission be integrated into your life? Close your time of reflection with a specific prayer about submission as a discipline of spiritual growth for you.

Day Three: *The Cross Style*

> Have this mind among yourselves, which is yours in Christ Jesus, who, though he was in the form of God, did not count equality with God a thing to be grasped, but emptied himself, taking the form of a servant, being born in the likeness of men. And being found in human form he humbled himself and became obedient unto death, even death on a cross. Therefore God has highly exalted him and bestowed on him the name which is above every name, that at the name of Jesus every knee should bow, in heaven and on earth and under the earth, and every tongue confess that Jesus Christ is Lord, to the glory of God the Father.
>
> —Philippians 2:5–11

This is one of the most beautiful descriptions of Jesus. More clearly than any place else in scripture, the shape of the incarnation is described here: humiliation, weakness, and obedience. There is a cryptic expression of it in Second Corinthians 8:9: "For you know the grace of our Lord Jesus Christ, that though he was rich, yet for your sake he became poor, so that by his poverty you might become rich."

For me, Philippians 2:5–11 is the greatest and most moving passage anyone ever wrote about Jesus. But not only is it a vivid description of who Jesus is, it is a call to us. "Let this mind be in you, which was also in Christ Jesus: who . . . took upon him the form of a servant . . . and became obedient unto death, even the death of the cross" (KJV).

We will come back to this later, but note this now: *One of the purposes of the discipline of submission is to cultivate the mind of Christ in us.* But let's stay with our focus now.

The foremost symbol for all Jesus was and did is the cross. The cross is the symbol for his most radical expression of submission and servanthood. But don't miss the larger truth. Golgotha's cross is the climax, the dramatic, final expression of Jesus' self-giving. But it only climaxed there. And what climaxed there on that black day that became Good Friday for us was a way of life at the center of which was always a cross.

Jesus' way was the way of the cross, and this was essential to his ministry. He chose the way of humiliation (he "emptied himself," refusing to hang on to the glory that was his with the Father). He reversed all notions of greatness and power (he became weak that we may be strong, poor that we may be rich). And he chose obedient submission even to death on the cross.

So, his was a cross-way of life, which made his teaching the most revolutionary in history. His call was to a cross style of life. "And he called to him the multitude with his disciples, and said to them, 'If any man would come after me, let him deny himself and take up his cross and follow me' " (Mark 8:34). He minced no words: "And he sat down and called the twelve; and he said to them, 'If any one would be first, he must be last of all and servant of all' " (Mark 9:35).

Perhaps the most dramatic witness of this cross style was his action at the last supper with his disciples in the Upper Room. No one was around to perform that common act of a servant when persons came in off the hot dusty roads—washing feet. This was a borrowed room, thus there was no servant or head of the house or anyone to see that the menial task was performed. Jesus provided the unforgettable picture of submission, of the cross style, by washing the disciples' feet. Lest the ongoing meaning of this be lost in the bafflement of what was happening, Jesus made it clear.

> After washing their feet and taking his garments again, he sat down. "Do you understand," he asked, "what I have done for you? You call me 'Master' and 'Lord', and rightly so, for that is what I am. Then if I, your Lord and Master, have washed your feet, you also ought to wash one another's feet. I have set you an example: you are to do as I have done for you."
> —John 13:12–15, NEB

Voluntary submission, freely accepted servanthood—this is the cross style of life to which we are called.

Reflecting and Recording

In memory now, get in touch with a recent experience in which you expressed the cross style by your actions and/or attitudes. Record that experience here. Write enough to get it clearly in mind. You don't have to use complete sentences, but be specific in naming persons, circumstances, details of actions, words, attitudes.

Now pull from that memory, as much as possible, feelings that you had at the time. Put down single words that express those feelings.

Try to be in touch as much as possible with your feelings, as well as the event itself. Would it be worth it to make such happenings more common in your life?

If your answer is *yes,* reflect for two or three minutes on why you resist this style.

If your answer is *no,* look again at the experience, and ask if what you did in the situation was close to your imagining of what Jesus might do. And if that is true, wrestle with the fact that actions you feel are not worth making more common in your life may be the kind of actions Jesus is calling for.

Pray however you are led in response to your consideration of Jesus' call to a cross style.

Day Four: *Practicing Submission*

In *Celebration of Discipline,* Richard Foster lists seven acts of submission which provide a guide for practicing submission.

To the Triune God. ''In the name of the Father, and of the Son, and of the Holy Spirit'' is not just the closing salutation of our prayer, it is the grounding of our lives as Christians. The purpose of all spiritual disciplines is that we may say "yes" to God in all our life every day. So we begin the day waiting before the Father, Son, and Holy Spirit. In a deliberate, self-conscious, purposeful way, we yield our body, mind, and spirit to God. We then seek to move through the day in submission to God, praying to be guided by the Spirit to express the mind of Christ in all our doings. We close the day in submission. All we have experienced—failures and accomplishments, sins and deeds of mercy—we surrender to God, and wait on him unconsciously through the night for rest and renewal.

To the Scripture. No discipline is more vital for spiritual growth than living with scripture. Thus responding obediently to scripture is central in the discipline of submission. We are to practice hearing, receiving, and obeying the word. As an ongoing part of our life we need to hear the word preached and taught in worship and study settings. We also need to develop our own devotional use of scripture. Living with the Bible *devotionally* equips us to be more receptive to the word preached and taught. Scripture accomplishes God's purpose only as we act upon it, only as we obey. We practice submission by depending upon the Holy Spirit who inspired the word to interpret the word and give us the insight to apply it to our condition, as well as the power to act upon it in our daily lives and relationships.

To Our Family. In this most intimate arena, submission is most desperately needed, tried, and tested. What Paul said to the Philippians has special relevance to the family: "Let each of you look not only to his own interests, but also to the interests of others" (Phil. 2:4). Two keys to submission in the family are listening and caring. We listen because we care, and we can give practical expression to our caring by listening.

To Our Neighbors and Those We Meet in the Course of Our Daily Lives. Ordinary neighborliness—simple acts of kindness and expressions of concern—is still a great need. To be willing to "put ourselves out" a bit, to go out of our way to express caring, is one of the essential ways of practicing submission. Little acts that require limited time and energy but call for an act of the will train us for the demanding work of submission.

To the Church. When Paul was dealing with the controversy that had arisen in the Corinthian church over the exercise of spiritual gifts, he said, "Since you are eager for manifestations of the Spirit, strive to excel in building up the church" (1 Cor. 14:12). Since the church is the body of Christ in the world, we must do our part to see that the cross style is present in relationships among her members, in the way we respond to the needs of each other, in the way we order our lives, and in the way we serve. Even the seemingly mundane matters of organization, committee work, the ongoing routine such as ushering and serving meals, can be acts of submission. Certainly evangelistic visitation, hospital calls, life together in study and prayer groups, teaching Sunday school, and singing in the choir can be dynamic expressions of the cross style.

To the "Least of These." Here the call to submission is really tested in what we do and how we care for those Jesus called "the least of these": widows, orphans, prisoners, the sick, the poor, the oppressed—all those who are forced to live on the fringes in life, out of the main stream. We are called to act on behalf of those who can't reciprocate in any sort of "you scratch my back, I'll scratch yours" approach to life. A confession of a temptation will illustrate.

I am the Senior Minister of a 3,700-member congregation. We have a number of ordained clergy and other professional persons on our staff, each assigned specific areas of responsibility. Though we have two clergymen who have hospital visitation as a part of their responsibility, I try to make hospital calls at least one afternoon a week. My temptation, given my limited time, is to visit only the "leadership" of our church who are hospitalized. To combat this temptation I deliberately select the hospital in which we have the most members on the day that I'm calling, or the place where there is a particularly crucial pastoral need, and I visit every member who is there, many whom I have not had the opportunity to know personally.

Now this may sound small, but it reflects a basic problem. Our temptation is to serve those who can serve us, those with whom there may be some "payback." Jesus knew, so he called us to minister to the "least of these."

To the World. "Global village" as a description of our world is not a romantic notion, it is a statement of fact. We are internationally interdependent. Community, state, or national isolation is suicidal. How we live affects how others may live. It has been said that we must live simply that others may simply live.

Environmental concern, food consumption, financial stewardship, political involvement, generosity to others are acts of submission that can express concern and make a difference in the world.

Reflecting and Recording

An Inventory. Move through each of these areas of concern and make some notes about how you are currently practicing submission. Then select two areas to which you want to give special attention for the next few weeks. Make some specific decisions and plans for practicing submission in those areas. Record those decisions and plans as an act of commitment.

The Triune God

The Scripture

The Family

Neighbors and Those We Meet in the Course of Our Daily Lives

The Church

The "Least of These"

The World

Perhaps you would like to establish a plan to deal specifically with each of these areas. One way to do this would be to work on a couple of areas at a time, assigning a time frame such as a couple of weeks or a month to give them particular attention. Then move to other areas of concern.

The purpose of discipline is to work in such a consistent way, and with such a focus, that what we do for a time by deliberate and disciplined effort will eventually become spontaneous. This is especially so with a discipline such as submission. If you desire to make such a plan for focusing on these areas of submission, put dates beside each area of concern as a commitment to a time frame.

Lodge this scripture solidly in your mind to hold you to the decision you have made to focus on a particular area of submission. If you do not know it "by heart," memorize it or copy it on a piece of paper to carry with you into the day. Repeat it to yourself, or read it as you approach an occasion or relationship calling for submission.

> I appeal to you therefore, brethren, by the mercies of God, to present your bodies as a living sacrifice, holy and acceptable to God, which is your spiritual worship.
>
> —Romans 12:1

Day Five: *Servants after the Style of Jesus*

The disciplines of submission and serving go together. It is inevitable that a stance of submission leads to a style of serving. We practice submission in order to become servants after the style of Jesus. Ponder again Paul's description of Jesus. Go back to Day Three of this week and read Philippians 2:5–11 with which that day began.

Now get another scriptural picture in mind, the picture from the Upper Room where Jesus was eating the Passover meal with his disciples.

> Jesus, knowing that the Father had given all things into his hands, and that he had come from God and was going to God, rose from supper, laid aside his garments, and girded himself with a towel. Then he poured water into a basin, and began to wash the disciples' feet, and to wipe them with the towel with which he was girded. He came to Simon Peter; and Peter said to him, "Lord, do you wash my feet?" Jesus answered him, "What I am doing you do not know now, but afterward you will understand." Peter said to him, "You shall never wash my feet." Jesus answered him, "If I do not wash you, you have no part in me." Simon Peter said to him, "Lord, not my feet only but also my hands and my head!" Jesus said to him, "He who has bathed does not need to wash, except for his feet, but he is clean all over; and you are clean, but not every one of you." For he knew who was to betray him; that was why he said, "You are not all clean."
>
> When he had washed their feet, and taken his garments, and resumed his place, he said to them, "Do you know what I have done to you? You call me Teacher and Lord; and you are right, for so I am. If I then, your Lord and Teacher, have washed your feet, you also ought to wash one another's feet. For I have given you an example, that you also should do as I have done to you. Truly, truly, I say to you, a servant is not greater than his master; nor is he who is sent greater than he who sent him. If you know these things, blessed are you if you do them."
>
> —John 13:3–17

It is clear as we read the New Testament that *serving* is the most distinctive quality of Jesus' style of ministry. And Jesus leaves little doubt that it is the style to which he calls us. "The disciple is not superior to his teacher, nor the slave to his master" (Matt. 10:24, JB). "Anyone who wants to be great among you must be your servant...just as the Son of Man came not to be served but to serve" (Matt. 20:26–28, JB). Not only does Jesus call us to this style, he gives life through this style: "Anyone who finds his life will lose it; anyone who loses his life for my sake will find it" (Matt. 10:39, JB).

It is clear. The style to which we are called is that of serving. But not many of us want to be servants, do we? Also, there is a vast difference between the way most of us serve and Jesus' call to be a servant.

> The way most of us serve keeps us in control. We choose whom, when, where, and how we will serve. We stay in charge. Jesus is calling for something else. He is calling us to be servants. When we make this choice, we give up the right to be in charge. The amazing thing is that when we make this choice we experience great freedom. We become available and vulnerable, and we lose our fear of being stepped on, or manipulated, or taken advantage of. Are not these our basic fears? We do not want to be in a position of weakness (Dunnam, *Alive in Christ,* p. 150).

Here is the conflict. Even though we make the decision to serve, undisciplined as we are, we continue to choose when, where, whom, and how we will serve. Thus we continually run the risk of pride and we are always vulnerable to a "good works" mentality that sends us frantically to engage ourselves in whatever deeds of mercy we can devise. How do we deal with these snares?

Pride. Thomas Merton reminds us that

> he who attempts to act and do things for others or for the world without deepening his own self-understanding, freedom, integrity and capacity to love, will not have anything to give others. He will communicate to them nothing but the contagion of his own obsessions, his agressiveness, his ego-centered ambitions, his delusions about ends and means (Merton, *Contemplation in a World of Action,* pp. 178–179).

If we think we know others and their needs perfectly well, our serving will often hinder rather than help. To combat pride, we must be attentive to the other—a form of submission—patient, intent on serving the genuine needs of the other, rather than serving our own need to serve. In this fashion we will diminish the possibility of being *on our own.* We will be open to the Spirit to guide us in discerning need and in making appropriate responses to need.

"Good Works" Mentality. Given a decision to serve, we think we must immediately spring into action. We must guard against two pitfalls. Our desire to serve may be poisoned by a desire to please. Also, there is the snare of turning our servant action into controlling power over another.

One antidote for a "good works" mentality is an ongoing sensitivity to our own unworthiness. The Bible witness is clear. Awareness of a calling to service is accompanied by a sense of personal unworthiness.

A "good works" mentality is also dissolved by keeping alive the conviction that our salvation is dependent upon God's grace, not our performance.

A third antidote to a "good works" mentality is an ongoing awareness that our serving is not redemptive within itself. Our serving provides the environment, sets the stage, and releases the energy for the person we are serving to be genuinely helped, even healed.

Now we return to the central issue. We discipline ourselves in serving, deliberately acting as servants, because we are servants of Christ. Thus our choosing to serve elicits no false pride.

In a disciplined way we choose and choose and decide and decide to serve here or there, this person or that person, now or tomorrow, until we take the form of a servant and our lives become spontaneous expressions of the cross style.

Reflecting and Recording

In the left column, list three specific occasions when you have served others in the past few weeks.

In the center column, describe those acts of service, what you felt your service was going to do for the person.

In the right column, note what pride you felt in what you were doing, and whether you were acting out of a "good works" mentality. In recording these feelings, try to recall whether you were conscious of guarding against pride and a "good works" mentality. Note whether any action would have been different had you been conscious of these antidotes.

1.

2.

3.

During the next few days observe your serving acts. Ask yourself these questions:

1. Am I serving a genuine need of this person, or serving my own need to serve?
2. Am I trying to please this person?
3. In my serving am I gaining any control?
4. Am I doing this in any way to gain "merit" for myself with God or with the persons served?

Pray for the gift of being critical of how you serve, yet for freedom to serve without being ponderous.

Day Six: *For What Purpose?*

Richard Foster makes a convincing case for the fact that every discipline has its corresponding freedom. In the introduction to this workbook, I contended that disciplines in themselves have little or no value. "They have value only as a means of setting us before God so that He can give the liberation we seek. The liberation is the end; the Disciplines are *merely* the means. They are not the answer; they only lead us to the Answer" (Foster, p. 96).

For what purpose is the discipline of submission? Let's look at two purposes. The first, in Foster's framework, is a freedom: the ability to lay down the terrible burden of always needing to get our own way. Let Foster state it.

> The obsession to demand that things go the way we want them to go is one of the greatest bondages in human society today. People will spend weeks, months, even years in a perpetual stew because some little thing did not go as they wished. They will fuss and fume. They will get mad about it. They will act as if their very life hangs on the issue. They may even get an ulcer over it (Foster, p. 97).

In the discipline of submission we are released to drop the matter, to forget it. Frankly, most things in life are not nearly so important as we think they are.

> If we could only come to see that most things in life are not major issues, then we could hold them lightly. We discover that they are no big deal. So often we say, "Well, I don't care," when what we really mean (and what we convey to others) is that we care a great deal. . . . The biblical teaching on submission focuses primarily on the spirit with which we view other people (Foster, p. 97).

So this is the first purpose—to lay down the terrible burden of always needing to get our own way, thus finding the freedom to value and serve others.

The second purpose of the discipline of submission is to cultivate the mind of Christ in us. Like all disciplines, we practice submission in order to be more open to God, more sensitive to God's presence, more discerning of God's will. Submission is a concrete expression of this desire.

For three days we have focused on Jesus, his life and his call to a cross style. Submission is a very practical way to cultivate that style, thus to have the mind of Christ made more dominant in us.

This second purpose of the discipline of submission enables us to identify and deal with the limits of submission. As indicated earlier, when distorted, submission can become destructive. The mind of Christ, with love as the signal characteristic, is the plumb line.

> Peter called Christians to radical submission to the state when he wrote, "Be subject for the Lord's sake to every human institution, whether it be the emperor as supreme, or to governors..." (1 Pet. 2:13, 14). Yet when the properly authorized government of his day commanded the infant church to stop proclaiming Christ, it was Peter who answered, "Whether it is right in the sight of God to listen to you rather than to God, you must judge; for we cannot but speak of what we have seen and heard" (Acts 4:19, 20). Upon a similar occasion Peter stated simply, "We must obey God rather than men" (Acts 5:29).
>
> Understanding the cross-life of Jesus, Paul said, "Let every person be subject to the governing authorities" (Rom. 13:1). When Paul, however, saw that the state was failing to fulfill its God-ordained function of providing justice for all, he called it to account and insisted that the wrong be righted (Acts 16:37) (Foster, p. 105).

These apparent contradictions of Peter and Paul express the truth: When it becomes destructive, submission is not only invalid as a spiritual discipline, it is contrary to the mind of Christ, his law of love.

Reflecting and Recording

List three situations in which the limits of submission are clear, such as when a citizen is asked to violate his or her Christian conscience and the dictates of scripture for the sake of the state.

1.

2.

3.

In your own life and in the lives of other persons you know, list (here and on the next page) three situations where the limits of submission are extremely difficult, almost impossible to define.

1.

2.

3.

This exercise makes plain the fact that there can be no "law of submission" which covers every relationship and situation. So we keep before us the mind of Christ, and we pray and live with scripture and counsel with our Christian friends, depending upon the Holy Spirit to provide discerning grace.

A big part of the discipline process is simply to *stay with it*. On Day Four you were asked to choose two areas of submission to which you would give focused attention. Did you? How is it coming? What opportunities have come along for you to practice that discipline in those areas?

Here is Phillips's translation of Colossians 1:27, which affirms the indwelling Christ. Memorize it now as an affirmation to guide you in submission.

> The secret is simply this: Christ *in you!* Yes, Christ *in you* bringing with him the hope of all the glorious things to come.

Pray that you will become more and more aware of the indwelling Christ and that your efforts at submission will not only serve others, but cultivate the mind of Christ in you.

Day Seven: *An Identifying Mark of a Servant*

We will consider further the discipline of serving in Week Six as we link serving with generosity. As a bridge let's consider today an identifying mark of a servant: *obedience*. Not only is obedience an identifying mark of a servant, it is the motivating power for submission.

Read again the story of Jesus washing the disciples' feet. The passage is included in Day Five on page 100. We will find in that story some informative truths about obedience. So read it now before you continue.

Now the truths from the story.

One. *Personal involvement is required of the obedient servant.* "If I then, your Lord and Teacher, have washed your feet, you also ought to wash one another's feet" (John 13:14). There is no way to serve *in absentia.* To be obedient always mean personal involvement.

No Christian movement or organization has demonstrated a more transparent obedient response to Christ in serving than the Salvation Army. In his last public address, in May 1912, the Army's founder, William Booth, gave a moving testimony which became his spiritual testament, for he died three months later. As quoted in *A Hundred Years' War: The Salvation Army 1865-1965* by Bernard Watson:

> While women weep as they do now   —I'll fight;
> while little children go hungry
>   as they do now   —I'll fight;
> while men go to prison, in and
>   out, in and out, as they do now   —I'll fight;
> while there is a drunkard left,
> while there is a poor lost girl
> upon the streets, while there
> remains one dark soul without
>   the light of God   —I'll fight
>   —I'll fight to
>   the very end!

The Salvation Army is a witness to the fact that obedience means personal involvement.

Two. *One cannot be obedient without Christlike unselfishness.* "For I have given you an example, that you also should do as I have done to you" (John 13:15).

Obedience never comes easily because it calls for unselfishness, and unselfishness goes against the grain of our pride, our desire for security, our trust in money and material things. Ruth Harms Calkin has put it well in *Tell Me Again, Lord, I Forget:*

> You know, Lord, how I serve You
> With great emotional fervor
> In the limelight.
> You know how eagerly I speak for You
> At a women's club.
> You know how I effervesce when I promote
> A fellowship group.

> You know my genuine enthusiasm
> At a Bible study.
> But how would I react, I wonder
> If You pointed to a basin of water
> And asked me to wash the calloused feet
> Of a bent and wrinkled old woman
> Day after day
> Month after month
> In a room where nobody saw
> And nobody knew.

Three. *Life and meaning come to those who obediently serve.* "If you know these things, blessed are you if you do them" (John 13:17).

Blessed. That's the word of the Beatitudes. "Happy are you" is a way to translate it. But that word is adequate only if we invest into it more than the surface good feeling, more than the "all is well" state of those who measure meaning by what they have, their physical and mental security, the absence of problems and conflict. Jesus is talking about deep meaning and life itself. J. B. Phillips makes the case, in *When God Was Man,* by altering the Beatitudes to fit our false notion of "happiness."

> Happy are the "pushers": for they get on in the world.
> Happy are the hard-boiled: for they never let life hurt them.
> Happy are they who complain: for they get their own way in the end.
> Happy are the blasé: for they never worry over their sins.
> Happy are the slavedrivers: for they get results.
> Happy are the knowledgeable men of the world: for they know their way around.
> Happy are the troublemakers: for they make people take notice of them (Phillips, pp. 26–27).

Jesus reverses all this and gives us life only for losing our lives for his sake and the gospel. To be blessed, as Jesus promises, is not to escape pain and suffering. It doesn't mean people won't take advantage of us. It means that we will have the ultimate joy of knowing that we are supported by Christ, affirmed and accepted by him, and that our lives have meaning in God's plan.

Let's go to the scripture again to gain perspective. Look at Paul as an obedient servant, submissive to Christ, "being given up to death for Jesus' sake" (2 Cor. 4:11); and submissive to and serving others, "so death is at work in us, but life in you" (2 Cor. 4:12). Now listen to him:

> We are afflicted in every way, but not crushed; perplexed, but not driven to despair; persecuted, but not forsaken; struck down, but not destroyed.
>
> —2 Corinthians 4:8–9

There are four words that tell clearly what sometimes happens to obedient servants after the style of Jesus: *affliction, perplexity, persecution,* and *rejection.*

Affliction here, as the original Greek term suggested, has in it the idea of pressure or stress brought on by difficult persons or circumstances.

Perplexity has the same meaning as confusion. The combination of Greek terms that comprised the original word means "without a way." It means uncertainty, not knowing where to turn or where to find help.

Persecution is just that, the experience of being aggressively punished, put down, intimidated, or discredited.

Rejection is the best word for the term "struck down." It is the idea of being shoved aside, disregarded in an explicit way; thus it denotes a form of persecution.

We close with a reminder from scripture that obedient service which flows out of submission may not be easy; in fact, it is very demanding. However, a word of caution needs to be stated. Don't go looking for affliction, confusion, rejection, and persecution. It is wrong to think that we are not serving the Lord unless we are suffering. We simply need to get perspective. The demands of serving are not easy, but the Lord is gracious and will equip us for the tasks to which he calls us. Also, we need to remember his word: "In the world you have tribulation; but be of good cheer, I have overcome the world" (John 16:33).

Reflecting and Recording

Spend some time now in reflection and prayer. Think about the call to submission, the responses and commitments you have already made. Are you happy with these responses and commitments? Are there others you need to make? Do you have a clear plan for following up on submission as a discipline for spiritual growth?

Group Meeting for Week Four

Introduction

Paul advised the Philippians to "let your conversation be as it becometh the gospel" (Phil. 1:27, KJV). Most of us have yet to see the dynamic potential of the conversation which takes place in an intentional group such as this. The Elizabethan word for *life* as used in the King James version is *conversation,* thus Paul's word to the Philippians. Life is found in communion with God and also in conversation with others.

Speaking and listening with this sort of deep meaning which communicates life is not easy. This week our emphasis has been on submission and service. To take conversation seriously is both submission and service. To listen is especially an act of submission. When we listen in a way that makes a difference, we surrender ourselves to the other person, saying, "I will hear what you have to say and will receive you as I receive your words." When we speak in a way that makes a difference we speak for the sake of others, thus we are serving.

In these weekly sessions, beginning at this one, see your participation in conversation as submission and service.

Sharing Together

1. Spend twenty to thirty minutes sharing the most significant insight or learning each person has received this week. Don't just *name* the insight or learning; talk about its meaning in your life, how it came, why you think it was for you this week. What is going on in your life to make this insight or learning relevant?

2. Ask someone to read the quote from *Alive in Christ,* on page 101. Spend ten to fifteen minutes talking about this understanding of serving. Am I right in defining Jesus' style in this fashion? Do we have much serving in this manner? Is such a style possible? To what degree is each of us seeking that style?

3. Turn to Day Seven of this week and review what sometimes happens to obedient servants after the style of Jesus. Let persons in the group share any such experiences they have had.

4. Let the entire group share in writing a definition of *Christian submission.*

Praying Together

Corporate prayer is one of the great blessings of Christian community. To affirm that is one thing; to experience it is another. To *experience* it we have to *experiment* with the possibility. While Jesus insisted that being alone with God is a basic dimension of prayer, we need to understand also the possibility of the mind and will of God becoming clear to us when we pray with others: "If two of you agree..." (Matt. 18:19).

Will you become a bit bolder now, and experiment with the possibilities of corporate prayer by sharing more openly and intimately?

1. Spend three minutes in quietness, asking yourself, "What are the things in my life that prevent me from practicing submission?"

2. Let each person share one barrier to submission in his or her life. (It will be helpful to take notes on this sharing, so you can pray for your friends in a more focused way.)

3. There is a sense in which, through this sharing, you have already been corporately praying. There is power, however, in a community on a common journey verbalizing thoughts and feelings to God in the presence of fellow pilgrims. Experiment with this possibility now.

> a. Let the leader call each person's name, pausing briefly after each name for some person in the group to offer a brief verbal prayer focused on what that person has shared. It should be as simple as, "Lord, give Jane victory over her fear of not being in control." (Leader, remember to call your own name.)
>
> b. When all names have been called and all persons prayed for, sit in silence for two minutes; be open to the strength of love that is ours in community. *Enjoy* being linked with persons who are mutually concerned.

4. On Day Four, you were asked to select two areas in which you would begin to practice submission. Let each person share aloud those two areas as an act of public commitment. When all have shared, again spend two minutes in silence praying for each other to find the will and wisdom to practice submission.

5. After the silence the leader may close the meeting by simply saying, "Amen."

You have two more weeks together as a group. By now, many groups feel the desire to continue as a group for a while. You may want to talk about this. You will find a list of suggested resources for your group at the back of this workbook.

Solitude

Day One: *Solitude and How We Use It*

Most of what has been written about solitude has been written from a Roman Catholic perspective. More narrow than that, it has been written from the perspective of the monastic life or the intentional religious community.

The common image is that of the austere monk spending most of his time alone in his cell; or more extreme, the religious hermit who has chosen to live completely alone, away from interaction with other persons, outside the physical presence of other people. What such persons do with their solitude may interest us and provide some helpful insights, but it is hardly the model most Christians would even consider pursuing.

It is significant to note that religious communities (and these are predominantly Roman Catholic) are intensely concerned about solitude and its function in their common life. Outside those communities we think that the rhythm of togetherness and solitude is balanced and enriching, that these persons have found a style that may be a model to inform us. But that is not always the case. As an introductory word to his discussion of the meaning of solitude for intentional Christian communities, Henri Nouwen wrote:

> It is in the midst of this dark world that the Christian community is being tested. Can we be light, salt, and leaven to our brothers and sisters in the human family? Can we offer hope, courage and confidence to the people of this era? Can we break through the

paralyzing fear by making those who watch us exclaim, "See how they love each other, how they serve their neighbor, and how they pray to their Lord"? Or do we have to confess that at this juncture of history we just do not have the needed strength or the generosity and that our Christian communities are little more than sodalities of well-intentioned people supporting each other in their individual interests? (Nouwen, pp. 8–9)

Then he made his claim that religious communities, bound together with the common vows of chastity, obedience, and poverty, are dependent in their life and witness upon a deep commitment to solitude.

Solitude is not only an essential discipline for those of religious orders who take vows of solitude, not only essential for those who live in community, it is a discipline for spiritual growth for all who wish to pursue the Christian life seriously.

As we begin our concentration on this discipline, focus on the obvious. When we talk about solitude as a discipline for spiritual growth, we are not thinking simply of aloneness or absence of involvement with others. Alfred North Whitehead in his book *Religion in the Making* provides the clue for meaning: "Religion is what a man does with his solitariness." More than aloneness is being spoken of here. When there is a religious dimension to solitude, we are not only physically apart from others, we are using aloneness purposefully. We are pondering who we are, what life is all about, where we are in our quest for meaning, and how we are related to God and others.

What we do with our solitude becomes the key. A letter of counsel credited to the anonymous writer of *The Cloud of Unknowing* provides guidance for us as we think of any discipline, especially the discipline of solitude.

> Silence is not God, nor speaking; fasting is not God, nor feasting; solitude is not God, nor company. . . . He lies hidden between them and no work of yours can possibly discover him save only your heart's love. Reason cannot fully know him for he cannot be thought, possessed or discovered by the mind. But loved he may be and chosen by the artless, affectionate longing of your heart. Choose him, then, and you will find that your speech has become silent, your silence eloquent, your fasting a feast, your feasting a fast, and so on. Choose God in love . . . for this blind thrust, this keen shaft of longing love will never miss the mark, God himself.

Reflecting and Recording

Look back over the past seven days. Make a list of the times you had at least thirty minutes alone, when you had nothing to do (other than your sleeping hours). List the day (Monday, Tuesday, etc.) and by each one the approximate time of day.

Now examine those times in terms of how you used them. Make some notes. Did you pray? Read? Try to busy yourself with some hobby? Feel that you were wasting time and should be doing something or talking to someone? Think about the ways you spend available time alone before you read further.

Recall the last occasion when you had one hour alone and spent it in silence, not reading or watching television or involved in some hobby or busy work. Does this say anything to you about how you are using your time?

As a discipline for the rest of this week, pick a time each day when you can spend at least thirty minutes in silence. You may want to add it to the time you spend using this workbook, or select some other specific time of each day. Go to that period of solitude and silence with only this workbook. The next page is blank. Use this blank page to record what you felt and experienced in your silence.

Close your time now with a prayer that God will enable you to discipline yourself in solitude and silence.

Notes on My Solitude and Silence

Day Two: *Increased Capacity for Discernment*

Yesterday we concluded our beginning thoughts about solitude by contending that the key to its religious meaning is what we do with it, how we use it. As a pastor, I have seen the havoc separateness and aloneness play in the lives of people. Whether forced or chosen, solitariness can be destructive. It can lead to despair. It can be a flight from life. It can evoke the final life-flight: suicide. The negative aspects of being alone lead persons to all sorts of destructive behavior: sexual promiscuity, indulgent consumption, total immersion in the crowd. These and other perverted activities and relationships are really efforts to be acceptable, stemming from a demonic passion to avoid separation and loneliness.

Our focus here is not upon forced or circumstantial solitude, though what we are saying here can apply to that experience. We are talking primarily about choosing and creating solitude for personal spiritual growth.

Solitude which is deliberately used for spiritual growth is a setting for an *increased capacity for discernment*. To be discerning we must be receptive and perceptive. In "Ash Wednesday," T. S. Eliot asked the probing question: "Where shall the word be found, where will the word resound?" And answered, "Not here, there is not enough silence." An old proverb says that the man who opens his mouth, closes his eyes. One purpose of solitude is to enhance our capacity to see and hear, to be receptive and perceptive, which is to discern.

One of my most memorable experiences was meeting and sharing for a day with Anthony Bloom, the Russian Orthodox priest who has written so helpfully on prayer and the contemplative life. Two of his books, *School for Prayer* and *Living Prayer*, are highly valuable. We were filming a conversation between Mr. Bloom and myself. I pressed him on the question of contemplative prayer. He completely disarmed me by summing up his understanding with a nursery rhyme he had learned in the United States.

> There was an old owl
> Who lived in an oak.
> The more he saw
> The less he spoke.
> The less he spoke
> The more he heard.
> Why can't we be like
> That wise old bird?

This is really the basis of the contemplative life, he insisted, to be alone enough, quiet enough, long enough that our jaded senses, dulled by the onslaught of a compulsive society, will be restored to aliveness. But more, to have enough solitude and silence that we might distance ourselves from all that clamors for our attention, and in that distancing gain perspective that enables us to see clearly, to be discerning, then to act intentionally with inspired intuition, rather than to react compulsively.

Reflecting and Recording

Here is a call to silence that reminds us of why the silence is needed.

> We must retire from all outward objects, and silence all desires and wandering imaginations of the mind; that in this profound silence of the whole soul, we may hearken to the ineffable voice of the Divine Teacher. We must listen with an attentive ear; for it is a still small voice. It is not indeed a voice uttered in words as when a man speaks to his friend; but it is a perception infused by the secret operations and influence of the Divine Spirit, insinuating to us obedience, patience, meekness, humility, and all the other Christian virtues, in a language perfectly intelligible to the attentive soul.... The external word, even of the gospel, would be an empty sound without this living fruitful word in the interior, to interpret and open it to the understanding (Fénelon, pp. 2–3).

Spend some time reflecting on your own experience of the "still small voice." Try to recall some specific experiences when, in silence, you may have heard "the ineffable voice of the Divine Teacher."

Day Three: *Solitude Is Essential for Prayer*

> When you pray, you must not be like the hypocrites; for they love to stand and pray in the synagogues and at the street corners, that they may be seen by men. Truly, I say to you, they have received their reward. But when you pray, go into your room and shut the door and pray to your Father who is in secret; and your Father who sees in secret will reward you.
> And in praying do not heap up empty phrases as the Gentiles do; for they think that they will be heard for their many words. Do not be like them, for your Father knows what you need before you ask him.
>
> —Matthew 6:5–8

The obvious lesson of this word of Jesus is two-fold. One, we must never allow prayer to be a self-display of piety. Two, prayer is far more than words; it is being with God, putting ourselves in his presence and seeking to be attentive to him.

Yet, is there more here? Jesus instructs us to be alone and pray. Is the closed door of our private room, or the "closet" as some translations have it, a synonym for solitude? Jesus' life was punctuated with deliberate times of chosen solitude. To inaugurate his ministry, he spent forty days in the desert (Matt. 4:1–11). He spent the entire night alone in the desert hills before he chose his twelve disciples (Luke 6:12). He sought the lonely mountain, with only three disciples, as the stage for the transfiguration (Matt. 17:1–2). He prepared for his highest and most holy work by a long night of prayer in the solitude of Gethsemane (Matt. 26:36–44).

He often connected significant acts of ministry or events in his life with a time of solitude. After miraculously feeding the five thousand, Jesus asked the disciples to leave, dismissed the crowd, and "went up on the mountain by himself" (Matt. 14:23). When the twelve had returned from a preaching and healing mission, Jesus told them, "Come away by yourselves to a lonely place" (Mark 6:31). "He withdrew to the wilderness and prayed," following the healing of a leper (Luke 5:12–16). When he received word of the death of John the Baptist, he "withdrew from there in a boat to a lonely place apart" (Matt. 14:13). And following a long night of work "in the morning, a great while before day, he rose and went out to a lonely place" (Mark 1:35).

Solitude was a regular practice with Jesus. Jesus called us to solitude because he knew that solitude was essential for prayer. Fénelon expressed this truth in a cryptic sentence: "How few there are who are still enough to hear God speak." Douglas Steere states the connection between prayer and solitude with a contemporary analogy.

> Prayer that transforms seems to require certain optimum conditions that tilt us towards its authentic practice and that clear the way in spite of the dispersion and the web upon web of preoccupations which tend to usurp our earthly life. When I go in to have my chest x-rayed each year, I am required to strip off my ordinary bodily coverings and to expose my chest to the piercing rays of this light. Solitude, solitariness, seems to express a similar preparatory readying function in its stripping me and preparing me for exposure to the radiant beams of love that the x-ray focus of prayer accomplishes (Steere, p. 90).

It was also Douglas Steere who shared with me a fresh translation of Hosea 2:14. He found it in Tokyo, on the wall of the meditation room of the Jesuit residence where William Johnston teaches and does much of his work in appropriating the resources of the East for Christian meditation. Written in Japanese characters on a scroll, it read: "I will entice you into the desert and there I will speak to you in the depths of your heart."

Solitude and prayer are linked in this call. When we are alone, away from the outer and inner barrage of distractions, shut off from the noisy din and frantic pace of activity and relationship, beyond the distractions of all the pulls upon our attention and energy, then we can be quiet enough to hear the divine whisper. So we seek solitude as a setting for prayer.

Not only can we hear God in the silence of solitude, there we can also be so settled and centered that we can speak to God out of the deepest feelings and needs of our lives. I have discovered that without solitude my praying is reduced to concern about surface issues, immediate happenings, present moment involvements. It is only when I carve out some daily time for solitude, if only thirty minutes, and add to that regular but less frequent times of three or four hours (usually weekly) that I stay in touch with my inner being and pray from my deepest feelings and needs.

A case in point. Recently, my oldest daughter Kim was married. She is the first of our three children to be married, therefore it has been a highly charged emotional experience. At the rehearsal Friday evening before the wedding on Saturday afternoon, I began to feel a kind of frantic desperation. This expressed itself in anxiety over the mechanics of the service, but was so pronounced that our church organist, a dear friend, noted it and expressed her loving concern.

The week had been hectic, our house crowded with people, and my schedule intense and booked to the minute. I had reserved no time for solitude. Saturday, the day of the wedding, I had a funeral at ten o'clock, so I took the three hours from seven to ten for solitude. I probed my depths, examined my feelings, reflected on my midlife situation as the first big *giving up* of a child was upon me, prayed for Kim and John, expressed gratitude for John as Kim's chosen life-mate. I went from that time of solitude to share in the funeral and move on to the wedding at 4:00 P.M., the reception and celebration with friends that didn't end until near midnight, with a relaxed centeredness and joy that I'm sure would not have been mine without that chosen solitude.

This does not mean that we cannot pray without some disciplined segments of solitude. There is a solitude of heart which can be maintained despite crowds and clatter. But rare is the person—in fact I don't know any such person—who can maintain inner attentiveness and heart-solitude in the midst of a busy life without being renewed by a solitude that is "beyond the grip on my surface self with all its plans and distractions" (Steere, p. 92).

Reflecting and Recording

The primary purpose of solitude is to be with God and to be with ourselves *with* God in a way that is not easy to any setting but is most difficult outside solitude. The purpose of silence is not just quietness but to enable us to listen. Silence that is a spiritual discipline is not simply refraining from talk, but listening to God. Catherine de Hueck Doherty has said this well.

> A day filled with noise and voices can be a day of silence, if the noises become for us the echo of the presence of God, if the voices are, for us, messages and solicitations of God. When we speak of ourselves and are filled with ourselves, we leave silence behind. When we repeat the intimate words of God that he has left within us, our silence remains intact (Doherty, p. 23).

Reflect on the thirty-minute periods of solitude and silence you have had thus far. Is there anything happening in that period that may add a different quality to the rest of your day?

It may be too early to ascertain any "quality" change, but it is the witness of countless persons who practice an ongoing discipline of solitude and silence that quality of life changes. We will consider some of those changes in the following days.

If you have not been reserving a daily time of solitude and silence apart from this time with the workbook, you may well ask yourself, why? Do you feel it will have no meaning? Are you too busy? Do you fear silence?

Close this time by dealing prayerfully with yourself and your attitude toward and your use of silence.

Day Four: *Sharpened Sensitivity to and Solidarity with Persons*

I have a friend, now eighty-six, who is a Trappist monk. He is one of the significant others in my life and has been a kind of spiritual guide for six years. I have spent only one full day with him personally, so our relationship is through a bond of prayer and the sharing of letters.

He has even become a part of our family, and occasionally he and my wife, Jerry, also correspond. My oldest daughter, Kim, sent him an invitation to her wedding, along with a letter which recounted her pilgrimage up to the point of choosing her mate. Kim received this letter from Brother Simon:

Dearest Kim:
How priceless a good to be invited by you to your June 18 wedding. Unhappy Simon—would that he could be there in person! None can deny that all the rest of him; heart, mind, soul, and imagination will be any place else on your great day, the eighteenth of June, when you are Mrs. John David Reisman, *Deo volente* forever.

The reading of your invitation hit me with a vague sense of loss. I questioned myself. Whence this sensitivity of possession? I took the problem across the corridor to a beautiful chapel to meet Jesus and let his Spirit speak to me while I just listened. The first word from Jesus was: "My Father suffered when I left him to marry my Divinity to your Humanity. As God I was still there with him in every way and where." You may go to Columbus, personally, to make a home for John David, but your divinity, received at Baptism and Confirmation, will always be present, and make itself experienced by your own dear loved ones down South in dear old Tennessee.

What about my feeling of possessing you? Remember Christ asked, "Who is my mother, my sister, my brother?" His own answer: "He who does the will of my Father." Not to boast, but I think you and I do just that; at least about 95%. So I am Jesus' brother; you are his sister, and therefore my sister also. Kim that was lost. Kim that will be, *sans pare*. Lucky John David! A doctor's wife is his "pragmatic" self. He forgets himself to identify with each and all of his patients. Coming home self-exhausted, your beauty of body, mind, and soul will be an emblem restoring his innate divinity.

I share the letter to make a big point. Though spending most of his life in silence and solitude, Brother Simon is in touch with life, sensitive to persons, perceptive about situations and events in an almost unbelievable way. It is obvious from such a witness as Brother Simon that one of the fruits of solitude is a sharpened sensitivity to and a solidarity with persons. In solitude and silence there comes a new freedom to be with people. We gain a capacity for a new attentiveness to the needs of others, a new responsiveness to their hearts. Thomas Merton observed:

It is in deep solitude that I find the gentleness with which I can truly love my brothers. The more solitary I am, the more affection

I have for them. It is pure affection, and filled with reverence for the solitude of others. Solitude and silence teach me to love my brothers for what they are, not for what they say. (Merton, *The Sign of Jonas,* p. 268).

Even accepting the truth of this testimony, we need to remember that simply being alone does not sharpen sensitivity and enhance solidarity. In our solitude we must open ourselves to the recreating power of quietness and stillness, the healing, sensitizing presence of Christ, so that coming out of solitude we can be with others meaningfully. In solitude we must settle ourselves inwardly, so that we will become aware of the indwelling Christ. It is the indwelling Christ who sharpens our sensitivity and makes us one with others.

Reflecting and Recording

Today, either now or when you go into your period of solitude and silence, use that time to cultivate awareness of the indwelling Christ. Take the workbook with you to follow this instruction:

- For three minutes repeat the Jesus prayer over and over again silently in your mind. "Lord Jesus Christ, Son of God, have mercy upon me a sinner."

- For the next five minutes let your mind and heart do what it will with that prayer.

- For three minutes, repeat this affirmation over and over again silently in your mind, putting your name in the blank. "_____, the secret is simply this: 'Christ *in you*! Yes, Christ *in you* bringing with him the hope of all the glorious things to come' " (Col. 1:27, Phillips).

- For five minutes let your mind and heart do what it will with that affirmation.

- For the balance of the time you have, imagine that Christ is walking with you through your waking day. In brief flashes imagine how you might encounter particular people, do particular things, engage in conversation with Christ there with you.

The compassion of Jesus was cultivated in solitude and expressed itself in specific ways.

And Jesus went about all the cities and villages, teaching in their synagogues and preaching the gospel of the kingdom, and healing every disease and every infirmity. When he saw the crowds, he had compassion for them, because they were harassed and helpless, like sheep without a shepherd. Then he said to his disciples, ''The harvest is plentiful, but the laborers are few; pray therefore the Lord of the harvest to send out laborers into his harvest.''

—Matthew 9:35–38

Commit yourself in prayer to cultivate the compassion of Christ in solitude and silence.

Day Five: *Solitude Enhances Creativity and Generativity*

Ralph Harper writes in *The Sleeping Beauty,* ''We know that serious things have to be done in silence. In silence men love, pray, listen, compose, paint, write, think, and suffer.'' This is a ministry of solitude in our lives: it enhances creativity and generativity.

I have discovered this in my life, especially in my writing. Much of what I have published in books and articles began not as ''something'' to be published, but as occasions of prayer and contemplation. I am not a formal journal keeper, though there have been time periods when I did keep a journal. Writing, however, has been one of my primary spiritual disciplines. Interestingly, when I am not alone, I can move into silence and solitude by writing better than any other way. I discovered this accidentally. For ten years my ministry with The Upper Room involved a lot of travel. Even on a crowded airplane with a person at either elbow, I found access to silence and solitude through writing.

The key is the focused attention writing requires. This focused attention enables us to escape the grip that noise and activity usually have on our minds. Thus there is a kind of emptying, beginning at the ''top,'' or the surface, then gradually moving deeper until we are at the center of ourselves.

That centering process may take place in any number of ways, which is what most of this workbook is all about, but writing has become for me a way of centering, of shutting out the clamor of my exterior world, and experiencing the restoration of interior solitude. This brings about an enhancement of creativity and generativity.

I resonate to the confession of Petru Dumitriu in *To the Unknown God:*

> A famous quotation, and a little-known one: ''Every word is the epitaph of a feeling''—it is by Nietzsche or La Rochefoucauld, I have forgotten which; and ''Theology is the subtlest form of atheism''—that is by a Viennese cafe metaphysician whom I know very well. I do not know if they are both right, but I know that I cannot go on for long talking about things that spring from the most intimate part of my being, from my ''heart'', as we call that central point of the computer, where the conscious mind coincides with the deepest depths; that I cannot go on talking a long time about what is most secret in me, without the spring running dry (Dumitriu, p. 242).

Solitude puts us in a *receiving* stance. Most of our days are filled with relationships, demands, requests, reactions, responses, noise, busyness, and movement. There is little or no harmony to it all. Each day is more erratic and episodic than ordered and consistent. Though we may not be self-consciously *giving,* time and energy are being taken from us.

In chosen solitude, we deliberately take a receiving stance. Moving beyond the surface and settling down into interior solitude, we not only are recreated in our natural gifts and being, we are energized by the love of Christ which unfolds these.

Many artists, writers, and musicians have witnessed to the fact that their creativity is dependent upon solitude. They paint, write, and compose out of their inner beings. But this is not the generativity and creativity most of us express (though there is more of the artistic genius in all of us than ever comes to the surface). Nor is this the creativity and generativity most of us want and need.

Isn't this our desire: to move through our days not as programmed and driven machines but as deciding, creating persons? Don't we want to be centers of spiritual power and harmony, signs of hope and peace to those around us, having at least hints of life infused with and empowered by a sense of the Divine Presence?

In *Amiel's Journal* for February 4, 1871, there is this word from Henri-Frederic Amiel:

> The lot is cast irrevocably. There are no more happy whole-natured men among us, nothing but so many candidates for heaven, galley-slaves on earth. . . . Duty seems now to be more negative than positive; it means lessening evil rather than actual good; it is a generous discontent, but not happiness; it is an incessant pursuit of an unattainable goal, a noble madness, but not reason; it is homesickness for the impossible, pathetic and pitiful, but still not

wisdom. The being which has attained harmony, and every being may attain it, has found its place in the order of the universe, and represents the divine thought at least as clearly as a flower or a solar system. Harmony seeks nothing outside itself. It is what it ought to be; it is the expression of right, order, law, and truth; it is greater than time, and represents eternity.

That "harmony" is a fruit of solitude and enables us to be creative and generative centers of self-propelling aliveness.

Reflecting and Recording

The big idea of our reflection today is that solitude and silence enhance creativity and generativity. If all our days are programmed to the minute, we are in danger of becoming not deciding persons but driven machines.

Spend about five minutes writing about yourself as a deciding person and/or a driven machine. Do this by expressing honestly what you do all day and why you do it. Be sure to state what you *feel* about all of it.

I shared my experience about writing serving to move me into solitude and silence, enabling me to move deeper into the center of my self. Did anything akin to this happen just now in your writing? Think about how and why it did or didn't.

We have talked about solitude and silence enabling us to be centers of spiritual power and harmony, signs of hope and peace to those around us. To what degree is that becoming a reality in your life?

How much more of a reality would you like it to be? What are you willing to do to make it so?

Are you recording your feelings about your daily times of solitude on the blank page provided in the workbook? You were asked to do that writing *following* your experience of solitude and silence. Today, and for the next two days, you may want to *begin* that time by writing what you feel as you come to that time. Be sure, though, to continue recording what you felt and experienced in your silence.

Close your time now by simply affirming, "_____, the secret is simply this: 'Christ *in you*! Yes, Christ *in you* bringing with him the hope of all the glorious things to come'" (Col. 1:27, Phillips). Pray as you are led.

Day Six: *A Time of Testing*

Then Jesus was led up by the Spirit into the wilderness to be tempted by the devil. And he fasted forty days and forty nights, and afterward he was hungry. And the tempter came and said to him, "If you are the Son of God, command these stones to become loaves of bread." But he answered, "It is written, 'Man shall not live by bread alone, but by every word that proceeds from the mouth of God.'" Then the devil took him to the holy city, and set him on the pinnacle of the temple, and said to him, "If you are the Son of God, throw yourself down; for it is written, 'He will give his angels charge of you,' and 'On their hands they will bear you up, lest you strike your foot against a stone.'" Jesus said to him, "Again it is written, 'You shall not tempt the Lord your God.'" Again, the devil took him to a very high mountain, and showed him all the kingdoms of the world and the glory of them; and he said to him, "All these I will give you, if you will fall down and worship me." Then Jesus said to him, "Begone, Satan! for it is written, 'You shall worship the Lord your God and him only shall you serve.'" Then the devil left him, and behold, angels came and ministered to him.

—Matthew 4:1–11

Martin Buber was once being asked by an audience a series of grandiose-sounding questions. Finally he burst out, "Why don't we ask each other the questions that come to us at three o'clock in the morning as we are tossing on our beds?" Thoreau contended that we can learn more about ourselves in a sleepless night than by a trip to Europe.

Solitude, whether chosen or forced upon us, is a time of testing. Jesus, led by the Spirit into the wilderness, is our classic witness of this. That forty days of solitude was his final preparation for his public ministry. There he wrestled with the devil in a life-death struggle. Who he was as messiah and the shape of his ministry were beaten out on the anvil of attractive, enticing temptation. Three times the devil tempted Jesus to accept the role of a popular, power-wielding messiah. That testing did not end, though Jesus was ultimately victorious. Luke's account of this temptation experience closes with this word: "And when the devil had ended every temptation, he departed from him until an opportune time" (Luke 4:13). The King James Version has it that the devil "departed from him for a season."

The inevitable presence of evil returned to test Jesus in Gethsemane. The option to evade those who would destroy him and escape death was there with overwhelming attractiveness. The depth of Jesus' agony in testing is seen in the bloody sweat that poured from him.

So solitude brings testing. We should see this not as something to evade. Though we do not invite the testing, there is a sense in which we may welcome it. We may welcome it if we go with God into solitude. Or, in the case of involuntary solitude such as that brought by grave illness, if we have known the presence and power of the living Christ in other times and can hold on, however tentatively, to his promise that he will "come again," that he will be with us "even to the end of the age," then we can welcome the testing that is coming to us in solitude.

Matthew closes his story of Jesus' wilderness temptation with the comforting assurance, "And behold, angels came and ministered to him" (Matt. 4:11).

Reflecting and Recording

Search your own memory to see if you can locate an experience of testing that came in solitude. If so, describe that experience. Write enough to express the circumstances, the nature of the testing or temptation, and your feelings at the time of the experience as you can recapture them.

Looking at that experience, try to assess how you dealt with it. Did you try to evade it? Get out of the solitude as quickly as possible to avoid dealing with it? Seek to occupy yourself or fill your mind otherwise so the "testing" might go away? Did you share it with someone else? Make notes here about your response.

It is clear in the Gospels that Jesus never tried to dismiss the fact of evil or diminish the power of evil in tempting and testing us. One of the petitions in the prayer he taught the disciples was "Lead us not into temptation, but deliver us from evil." Jesus did not try to explain evil away. He recognized the fact of it and dealt with evil by living with its reality, wrestling with it within himself, and by so doing he transformed it. He promised us himself, as the Holy Spirit, indwelling us to provide us the power to overcome temptation and transform our testing.

Out of the testing that comes in solitude we may emerge with purer understanding of our strength and weakness, a clearer perception of the passions of our lives and the deeper affections that dominate us at the core of our being. We may be purged of perverted desires and cleansed of the guilt and ugliness we feel for the perversion of those drives and instincts God has given us and called good. There may come an integration of different facets of our being that vie for dominance.

Two things are to be remembered. One, we may need to seek help outside our solitude. We may need a trusted friend, a pastor, or a counselor to assist us in dealing with the testing that has come. Two, we must never forget that "he who is in you [Christ] is greater than he who is in the world [evil-the-devil]" (1 John 4:4).

Day Seven: *Facing Death*

> I have never been anywhere but sick. In a sense, sickness is a place...where there's no company, where nobody can follow. Sickness before death is a very appropriate thing and I think those who don't have it miss one of God's greatest mercies (O'Connor, p. 163).

What is Flannery O'Connor saying about sickness and death? How do you feel about what she is saying? Write your response in four or five sentences.

Flannery O'Connor, from Milledgeville, Georgia, was one of the great contemporary southern writers. As a Roman Catholic and an ardent Christian, her fiction is a marvelous vehicle of faith and truth. She was an invalid most of her life, but she rarely mentions sickness or suffering. Aside from the letter from which the above passage comes, she never spoke of her own life being more afflicted than anyone else's.

Reread her tough but instructive word. Look at two truths in her word.

One, "sickness is a place." What does she mean? Sickness is something that happens to you—yes, but more. It can be a place where you think deeply, feel beyond yourself, identify with the suffering of others, deal with the fact of your own death, contemplate the cross and the meaning of One who suffered on your behalf.

Two, "a place where there's no company." None can follow you into suffering. They can be with you, but they can't be sick for you. They can identify with you and seek to suffer vicariously, but only you can do your suffering.

Sickness as a place, and as a place where there's no company, is an experience of solitude with the potential of opening us more fully to God and leading us to yield ourselves more completely to him. We do not choose the solitariness of the aged persons most of whose friends have died, or the solitude of serious illness, or an injury that lifts us out of the mainstream of life. In another category, we don't will the solitude of those three or four hours of sleeplessness that come at one or two o'clock in the morning, what Friedrich von Hügel called his "white nights." Yet, we can choose our response to this imposed solitude.

We may certainly use this time to face death—our own.

> Søren Kierkegaard, as a Christian existentialist, dedicates his powerful devotional classic *Purity of Heart* to "That Solitary Individual." In it he does his best to cut man off from refusing to face the prospect of his own death in the course of his flight from God. Kierkegaard believed that only as man came to the end of himself and recovered a condition of solitariness, of being taken into the desert, could he be brought into the transforming presence of God, who alone could both individuate and tender him. Kierkegaard strikes at man's attempt to escape solitude and to hide from God by plunging into the *crowd*. The *crowd* for him is the opposite of solitariness. If, throughout his life, a person has succeeded in depending upon soft companionship, abundant advice, the group, the crowd, Peer Gynt's "middle way," and has managed always to succeed in insulating himself from solitude by being constantly in the company of others, Kierkegaard points out that in death, at least, he will be confronted by what it means to be a "solitary individual." At this frontier the path narrows and all must travel Indian file. Death isolates, and before the prospects of death all props are withdrawn; all leaves cancelled; all makeup is removed and one's individual being is brought into view (Steere, p. 97).

Jesus himself did not escape the solitude of death. Gethsemane was the climax of his facing head-on what was always lurking around the corners of his life.

> And they said, "Look, Lord, here are two swords." And he said to them, "It is enough."
> And he came out, and went, as was his custom, to the Mount of Olives; and the disciples followed him. And when he came to the place he said to them, "Pray that you may not enter into temptation." And he withdrew from them about a stone's throw, and knelt down and prayed, "Father, if thou art willing, remove this cup from me; nevertheless, not my will, but thine, be done." And when he rose from prayer, he came to the disciples and found them sleeping for sorrow, and he said to them, "Why do you sleep? Rise and pray that you may not enter into temptation."
> —Luke 22:38–46

Jesus' wrestling with death in solitude did not end in Gethsemane. On the cross, he felt devastatingly alone and cried, ''My God, my God, why hast thou forsaken me?'' (Mark 15:34, KJV).

In the prospect of death, the depth of life is revealed. Our priorities, commitments, and values are tested. Whether imposed or voluntary, solitude can serve that purpose. What O'Connor said of sickness—that before death it is ''a very appropriate thing and . . . those who do not have it miss one of God's great mercies''—can also be said of solitude that comes in other ways than through sickness.

Douglas Steere has shared the witness of William Sullivan, a spiritual leader of a generation ago, who expressed the debt he owed to his early Roman Catholic seminary training in the use of solitude:

> There is no species of training that I ever underwent to which I owe more than to the habit of regular periods of inner solitude. Solitary we must be in life's great hours of moral decision; solitary in pain and sorrow; solitary in old age and going forth to death. Fortunate the person who has learned what to do in solitude and brought himself to see what companionship he may discover in it. What fortitude, what content. By a great blessing I had an aptitude for these hours of quiet reflection and grew to love them. . . . To be alone and still and thoughtful bestowed upon me the richest joy I knew and for this priceless cultivation I shall be thankful always (Steere, p. 99).

Unlike Sullivan I do not have an aptitude for solitude. It has taken me years to know how essential this discipline is for me. I have not yet grown to ''love'' these hours of quiet reflection; and I cannot yet claim for myself the ''richest joy'' that solitude bestows. I can't talk that glowingly. But I can witness to the benefit and the necessity with conviction. My life and ministry are being invested with a depth and quality that I know is connected with the discipline of silence and solitude.

Reflecting and Recording

Somewhere along the way, if not already, you will be alone, forced by illness or accident into a ''place'' and/or an experience into which no one can enter with you. What you do with that will determine what it does to you. And what you do now, in preparation for the inevitable, will be a determining factor.

It may be that you will want to make some specific decisions about your use of solitude. Use this guide to do so.

In the left column below, list the time or times during each day when you are alone. In the center column, designate how you currently use your time alone. In the right column, make notes as to how you might use the time more effectively in the future.

If you feel a need to have more deliberate solitude, look at your "normal" week, and determine the best time to set aside two or three specific periods of solitude. Maybe you could find a daily period of fifteen minutes or a weekly period of thirty minutes or an hour. Be specific and record those times as a commitment.

Now, go back and read the notes you made in response to your daily solitude and silence time. Let what you have experienced shape your praying as you close this special focus on solitude and silence.

In the introduction I suggested that you plan a retreat sometime soon after this week's involvement. If you are ready to have a retreat of silence—at least three hours, perhaps even a day—look at your calendar now and decide when you will do it. Write the date down as a commitment to be broken only in an emergency.

Group Meeting for Week Five

Introduction

This workbook is only an elementary introduction to disciplines for spiritual growth. This week we have emphasized solitude and silence. Like all disciplines the "work" of this one in our lives is cumulative. It will take some time of practice to feel its power in our lives.

It was suggested at the beginning that the group may want to have a retreat together. If you haven't worked out those plans do so tonight.

Sharing Together

1. Begin your time together by singing a chorus or hymn everybody knows.

2. Not only is private solitude and silence necessary and meaningful, corporate silence can also have great value. Quaker worship is centered in silence. Spend ten minutes in silence, with each person affirming the indwelling Christ and the presence of Christ in the relationship.

3. Now talk about what you experienced in the silence.

4. Let each person share his or her most meaningful day this week.

5. Now share the most difficult day. Talk about *why* the day was difficult.

6. Days Six and Seven focused on testing and death. Let those who have had such experiences share them and the learnings from them with the group, especially the kind of experience you were asked to recall on Day Six.

Praying Together

1. Begin your time of specific praying by thanksgiving. Let each person offer a sentence prayer, "Lord, I thank you for _____." Each person completes the prayer by naming something that is giving meaning and joy to that person.

2. Now enter a time of praise. In thanksgiving we express our gratitude for something that has come to us, some gift from another or

from God. Praise goes one step beyond thanksgiving. We *thank* God for what he has done; we *praise* him for who he is. The psalmist praised God in ways such as this: "Bless the Lord, O my soul; and all that is within me, bless his holy name!" (Psalm 103:1) Let persons offer their individual expressions of praise to God.

3. Confession is a key to prayer and is an important discipline for spiritual growth. Spend three minutes in a silent examination of conscience as we explored earlier.

4. Corporate confession is also important. Enter into a period of corporate confession, allowing as many as are led to offer a brief verbal prayer that will reflect a degree of corporate confession, recalling what has been shared during this time about fears and failures.

5. Close by sharing the Lord's Prayer together.

Generosity

Day One: *Giving Ourselves to God*

> The kingdom of heaven is like treasure hidden in a field, which a man found and covered up; then in his joy he goes and sells all that he has and buys that field.
>
> Again, the kingdom of heaven is like a merchant in search of fine pearls, who, on finding one pearl of great value, went and sold all that he had and bought it.
>
> —Matthew 13:44–46

This is Jesus' word about possessing the kingdom, and the teaching is clear. We must be willing to "sell all" to *own* (enter) the kingdom. The treasure hidden in the field which we stumble upon, or the pearl which we avidly seek—the kingdom is ours when everything else takes second place to it.

Juan Carlos Ortiz has put the truth in a modern parable.

> "I want this pearl. How much is it?"
> "Well," the seller says, "it's very expensive."
> "But, how much?" we ask.
> "Well, a very large amount."
> "Do you think I could buy it?"
> "Oh, of course, everyone can buy it."
> "But, didn't you say it was very expensive?"
> "Yes."
> "Well, how much is it?"
> "Everything you have," says the seller.
> We make up our minds, "All right, I'll buy it," we say.

"Well, what do you have?" he wants to know. "Let's write it down."

"Well, I have ten thousand dollars in the bank."

"Good—ten thousand dollars. What else?"

"That's all. That's all I have."

"Nothing more?"

"Well, I have a few dollars here in my pocket."

"How much?"

We start digging. "Well, let's see—thirty, forty, sixty, eighty, a hundred, a hundred twenty dollars."

"That's fine. What else do you have?"

"Well, nothing. That's all."

"Where do you live?" He's still probing.

"In my house. Yes, I have a house."

"The house, too, then." He writes that down.

"You mean I have to live in my camper?"

"You have a camper? That, too. What else?"

"I'll have to sleep in my car!"

"You have a car?"

"Two of them."

"Both become mine, both cars. What else?"

"Well, you already have my money, my house, my camper, my cars. What more do you want?"

"Are you alone in this world?"

"No, I have a wife and two children. . . ."

"Oh, yes, your wife and children, too. What else?"

"I have nothing left! I am left alone now."

Suddenly the seller exclaims, "Oh, I almost forgot! You yourself, too! Everything becomes mine—wife, children, house, money, cars—and you too."

Then he goes on. "Now listen—I will allow you to use all these things for the time being. But don't forget that they are mine, just as you are. And whenever I need any of them you must give them up, because now I am the owner" (Ortiz, pp. 34–35).

Farfetched? Well, read the parables of the kingdom again. And listen to this terrible word of Jesus: "If any one comes to me and does not hate his own father and mother and wife and children and brothers and sisters, yes, and even his own life, he cannot be my disciple. . . . So therefore, whoever of you does not renounce all that he has cannot be my disciple"(Luke 14:26, 33).

Tough? Yes, very!

Jesus dealt with possessions in a radical way because he knew that our possessions too often possess us. It is a sign of our "original sin" that we are possessive. The unconverted self, the ego (by nature it seems) is in bondage to things, slavishly persistent in acquiring and keeping. Apparently one of our natural instincts is *acquisition*. Children have to be taught to share. Owning and holding, not giving, are natural traits.

So the discipline of generosity is essential for spiritual growth. Because the acquiring and holding aspects of our being are so tenacious, generosity must begin with the giving of ourselves. Paul captured this succinctly in Second Corinthians 8:5. Tomorrow we will consider the entire passage in which this verse is set. But for now, this is the heartbeat of generosity: "First they gave themselves to the Lord."

Reflecting and Recording

As an inventory of your "all," read again the modern parable. By each item that the fellow named, i.e., "ten thousand dollars in the bank," make a note of your similar possessions. Stop when you get to the "two cars"; in the margin at that point list other "things" you own, other valuables, possessions. Then read on.

When you have finished reading and recording, sit quietly in prayerful reflection about what this parable means in your life.

Day Two: *A Pattern of Giving*

Albert Day has well reminded us that at no place do the lives of saintly people bear a clearer witness than in the discipline of generosity. Evelyn Underhill said that the saints she knew in the flesh were often quite unable to keep anything for themselves.

So important is the role possessions play in our lives, and so powerful a force are our attitudes toward and our handling of possessions and material wealth that many ardent Christians have assumed the vow of poverty. The monastic movement in Roman Catholicism was in part a response to the undermining role "things" play in efforts at spiritual growth. So the vow of poverty is a central monastic vow.

Quite evidently that vow is not appropriate or possible for all Christians. Material poverty may be the calling and vocation of some, but certainly not of all. That, however, does not diminish, but increases the need for the disciplines of generosity.

As indicated earlier when we considered submission, every discipline has its accompanying freedom. Generosity frees us from a raw possessive ego and also from our bondage to security in material things. Albert Day has spoken clearly on this issue.

> The ego is strongly possessive. Its possessiveness is revealed in all its relationships. Psychologists used to talk about the instinct for acquisition. Instincts are not so much in caste as they used to be. But acquisitiveness remains, whether as instinct or behavior pattern or inherited tendency or what have you?
>
> Left to itself, the ego is persistent in acquiring and in keeping. Sharing is not one of its passions.
>
> It is possessive of things—and has to be taught to give. Often it gives only under social compulsion. It gives because giving is good business or good social strategy. . . .
>
> No, giving is not a trait of the ego. Owning is! "Mine" is its dearest adjective. "Keep" is its most beloved verb!
>
> The ego is possessive. Its possessiveness in property manifests itself as stinginess, miserliness, greed. Its possessiveness of people makes jealous friends, husbands, wives, parents.
>
> Most persons who are possessive never recognize the fact. So complete is the domination of the ego that it is unconscious. It just seems natural. It is natural in the sense that it is characteristic of our perverted egocentric nature. It is not natural in the sense that it is characteristic of the nature God intended us to have and we may have by his grace.
>
> Because of this possessiveness of the ego, the practice of generosity is very significant. It is a denial, a repudiation of the ego. Faithfully practiced, generosity weakens the ego's authority. Every departure from the pattern the ego sets, makes the next variation easier. We are made that way (Day, p. 80).

With that perspective, let's look at a pattern of giving which we find in scripture. This focuses primarily on giving money. Since money is integral to our lives, how we give money usually is a reflection of our overall pattern of generosity.

> We want you to know, brethren, about the grace of God which has been shown in the churches of Macedonia, for in a severe test of affliction, their abundance of joy and their extreme poverty have overflowed in a wealth of liberality on their part. For they gave according to their means, as I can testify, and beyond their means, of their own free will, begging us earnestly for the favor of taking part in the relief of the saints—and this, not as we expected, but first they gave themselves to the Lord and to us by the will of God.
> —2 Corinthians 8:1–5

Here is a clear pattern of giving which instructs us.

One, they gave *liberally.* It helps to know that Paul was involved in collecting money for a hurting congregation in Jerusalem. The church is suffering there and as Paul travels in his evangelistic mission, he shares the needs of the Jerusalem Christians and receives an offering. Macedonia was an economically depressed area. The church there was as poor as the church in Jerusalem. Paul reflects on that: ''In a severe test of affliction, their abundance of joy and their extreme poverty have overflowed in a wealth of liberality.'' To underscore this emphasis on *liberality,* Paul says, they gave ''beyond their means.''

Two, they gave *voluntarily.* ''Of their own free will,'' Paul says. He goes even further. ''Begging us earnestly for the favor of taking part in the relief of the saints.'' Those Macedonians knew what it means to give. They knew that to share in the needs of others not only was a blessed relief for the recipient but a source of joy and meaning for those who gave.

Three, they gave *anonymously.* No single person or church is named by Paul. The churches in Macedonia, not First Church on the corner of Main and Fifth. Not James Wilkes and Susan Forbes, but the Christians of Macedonia.

I see nothing wrong about honoring people with our gifts or celebrating the memory of a person with our contributions. Yet, this calls for careful self-examination. We need to scrutinize our reasons for giving. Our giving is not an act of generosity if we give to bring attention to ourselves.

Four, they gave *joyfully.* Look at the strange way Paul put words together in ''their abundance of joy and their extreme poverty.'' Can it be? Joy and poverty together. From the perspective of those who put so much stock in material security and abundance as a source of happiness and meaning, this is a radical contradiction. Those of us who have never known, and will never know, real poverty will never know the depths of the truth that is in this contradiction. Yet, we need to continue to grapple with it. What we can know is *joyful* giving. It may well be that joyful giving comes only when we give not out of our abundance or surplus but sacrificially.

Reflecting and Recording

Examine your current pattern and the meaning of your giving by reflecting upon these questions.

What is the largest financial contribution you have made to any cause? Examine that experience of giving in light of the pattern we have just considered.

Was it a liberal gift in light of your potential?

Was it voluntary? Was any sort of coercion involved? Pressure?

Was it anonymous? If not, examine your motives for giving.

Was it joyful? Did you give it joyfully? Did joy come as a result of your giving?

Now another question: Of all the financial contributions you have ever made, what has been the most significant one in terms of joy and meaning to you? Examine that giving experience by using the same questions just asked in relation to your largest gift.

In reflecting upon and comparing these two experiences of giving, record here some learnings about generosity that have come clear to you.

Day Three: *Tithing—A Discipline of Generosity*

Tithing is the biblical pattern set for practicing generosity in the use of our money. The principle, which became a law in Judaism, began not in a focus on money but on all we possess: land, flocks, crops, even "bounty" out of war. To trace the biblical witness on tithing will give us the perspective we need to consider this principle as a discipline of generosity.

The story of the first offering in history is found in Genesis 4:3–7. This is the story of Cain and Abel making their offerings to God. The big issue in the story is that Abel's offering was acceptable to God but that Cain's was not. Why was this so?

It had to do with the quality of the offering. Abel gave the firstlings of his flock, while Cain's offering seems to have been an indiscriminate collection of the fruit of the ground.

The story in Genesis seems a bit confused as to the reason one offering was acceptable and the other not, but in the Epistle to the Hebrews there is this word: "By faith Abel offered to God a more acceptable sacrifice than Cain" (Heb. 11:4).

In the original story the meaning is difficult to comprehend. There is no indication why God preferred the gift of Abel to the gift of Cain. On the surface it seems quite arbitrary, and it seems that the whole business is unjust. Yet, when you live with it for a while at least this much comes clear: God requires the best we have to offer.

We move from that story of the first offering to the first mention of tithing in the Bible. This is in Genesis 14:18–20. It's the story of Abraham paying tithes to Melchizedek, who was a king of Salem as well as a priest of God. It was after Abraham had won a great battle.

Melchizedek blessed him and said, "Blessed be Abram by God Most High, maker of heaven and earth; and blessed be God Most High, who has delivered your enemies into your hand!" After receiving this blessing Abraham gave the priest a tenth of everything.

Now here the amount of the separated portion is designated for the first time. *It is the tenth*. It was a common practice among ancient warriors to tithe the spoils of war. Abraham, no doubt, was familiar with this custom. Yet, there was something different about this act of Abraham. It was an act of genuine devotion. He was worshiping the one true God and was giving to God the tenth of all he received. Therefore, it set the precedent of tithing.

The concept grows in the Old Testament and Jacob is the first person on record to enter into a tithing covenant with God. Listen to the record of that covenant in scripture.

> Then Jacob made a vow, saying, "If God will be with me, and will keep me in this way that I go, and will give me bread to eat and clothing to wear, so that I come again to my father's house in peace, then the Lord shall be my God, and this stone which I have set up for a pillar, shall be God's house; and of all that thou givest me I will give the tenth to thee."
>
> —Genesis 28:20–22

Now to be sure, there is something far less than Christian about such praying and such a relationship with God. God is not one to be bargained with. We don't make deals with him! He is not one from whom we can buy favors. He is not a godfather in the mafia sense or a cosmic bellhop in some grand hotel. Still the story of Jacob, and what Jacob is doing, though primitive and certainly not yet Christian, is something to reckon with.

When you read the story of Jacob rising early in the morning, going out and setting up an altar and praying to God as a result of what has happened to him, then the story speaks to us. You remember that Jacob had dreamed that a ladder was set between earth and heaven. Angels of God were ascending and descending the ladder. Jacob beheld the Lord standing above that ladder and the Lord spoke to him, offering great promises, climaxing with the affirmation, "Behold, I am with you and will keep you wherever you go, and will bring you back to this land; for I will not leave you until I have done that of which I have spoken to you" (Gen. 28:15). After awakening from that sleep, you will recall, Jacob uttered that famous witness, "Surely the Lord is in this place; and I did not know it" (Gen. 28:16).

When, in reflection, Jacob prays again and enters into that tithing covenant with God, it is on the basis of having received the promise from God. It is as though he is testing that promise and seeking to offer a response to it. That is certainly only the beginning of the development of the tithe in the history of the Hebrew people and in the Christian church, but it symbolizes the fact that *our relationship with God always involves giving to God a portion of that which he has already given us.*

It is this principle—returning to God a portion of that which he has blessed us with—that must be at the heart of our understanding of the tithe. Moses formulated that principle into law that all faithful Jews were to keep. That law was expressed at the close of the book of Leviticus, after many new statutes both moral and ceremonial had been given. The ancient law of the tithe was added as a constant reminder, and for preservation and emphasis. Listen to that principle stated as law:

> All the tithe of the land, whether of the seed of the land or of the fruit of the trees, is the Lord's; it is holy to the Lord. . . . And all the tithe of herds and flocks, every tenth animal of all that pass under the herdsman's staff, shall be holy to the Lord.
> —Leviticus 27:30, 32

After that final law the book of Leviticus closes with this word, "These are the commandments which the Lord commanded Moses for the people of Israel on Mount Sinai" (Lev. 27:34). So the precedent was set firmly in the fabric of Jewish life.

The classic and most dramatic warning came from Malachi. In language that is strong and unmistakable, this prophet pointed out that disobedience to the law of the tithe was the cause of Israel's apostasy in his day, and that reformation in this regard was the sure and only way to the restoration of the divine favor and blessing. Those words from Malachi are enough to cause us to know what the witness of the Old Testament is concerning the tithe. Consider it:

> Will man rob God? Yet you are robbing me. But you say, "How are we robbing thee?" In your tithes and offerings. You are cursed with a curse, for you are robbing me; the whole nation of you. Bring the full tithes into the storehouse, that there may be food in my house; and thereby put me to the test, says the Lord of hosts, if I will not open the windows of heaven for you and pour down for you an overflowing blessing.
> —Malachi 3:8–10

Reflecting and Recording

Tomorrow, we will consider how the discipline of tithing ministers to us. Reflect now upon your response to this biblical witness on tithing. Examine your pattern of giving in the context of this biblical call. Are you satisfied with your practice?

Day Four: *Tithing Provides Perspective and Enhances Performance*

For many Christians the precedent that is set for tithing in scripture is enough to lead them to a commitment to tithe. It should be so for all Christians if we are going to be people of "the book." There are other reasons, however, that merit consideration. Along with the teaching of scriptures two truths have kept me tithing for over thirty years.

One, tithing gives me *perspective*.

Giving my tithe to the Lord is an ongoing reminder of what money can and cannot do. Now it would be wrong to idealize poverty. And it would be equally wrong to caricature riches as though they were innately wrong. Having money can make an enormous positive difference in our lifestyles. But it is crucial to maintain *perspective* about the fact that there are certain things money cannot buy.

Money can't buy friendship. All up and down the economic ladder you will find persons seeking to buy friendship by giving gifts and doing deeds. And you will find persons in agony, haunted by intense feelings of loneliness, uncertain of the motives of those whose friendship they have sought to buy.

At a deeper level than this is the fact that money won't buy love. We have only to examine the media and public annals to uncover dramatic examples, even bizarre examples, of persons with money extravagantly seeking to purchase love. The less dramatic we never hear about. One of the most tragic persons I know is a friend who is not wealthy. In fact, she is now living on the brink of poverty, surviving by Social Security. All her life has been spent trying to buy love. The most painful result is that she is now sixty years old, and the one person who should be the enriching joy of her life, her son, is totally estranged from her. He sees her only when he must, driven to do so only when his conscience reminds him that, after all, she gave him birth. Money won't buy love.

And money won't buy respect. We may get some of our selfish wants by money. We may use it to gain loyalty and deference from others. But this loyalty and deference is a charade for respect and usually turns into contempt.

And money won't buy exemption from the problems which are common to everyone. Money or the lack of it doesn't keep children from breaking the hearts of their parents. Money or the lack of it doesn't prevent incurable diseases from ravaging our lives. Money or the lack of it is no key for holding marriages together. Money cannot shield us against the early death of a marriage partner and the loneliness that follows.

You see we don't buy character, meaning, and direction in life. We can't put peace of mind on our Visa cards. A sense of fulfillment, understanding, and wisdom are not in the arena where money is the medium of exchange. We can't purchase eternal life. Death is the great equalizer. I've never seen a hearse pulling a U-Haul trailer. Money can't purchase eternal life, but how we spend our money may rob us of eternal life. Jesus said, "Where your treasure is, there will your heart be also" (Matt. 6:21).

Two, tithing enhances my *performance* in the cause of God's kingdom.

Now if that sounds lofty, it really isn't. It's the most down-to-earth, practical thing I know. There are things that you and I can never do for Christ and the kingdom by ourselves. We have to be a part of a body, a community. This is especially true in the use of our money. I believe this is the primary reason that we are to bring all our tithes into the storehouse—into the church. The church can use that cumulative money to accomplish far greater things than we could ever accomplish on our own.

Reflecting and Recording

The prophet Malachi said, "Bring the full tithes into the storehouse, that there may be food in my house; and thereby put me to the test, says the Lord of hosts, if I will not open the windows of heaven for you and pour down for you an overflowing blessing" (Mal. 3:10).

Look at your own practice of giving money. What blessings have you received? Record them here.

Does the way you are giving money as an act of generosity provide perspective for you? How? Be specific. Record your thoughts.

Recall some accomplishment in which you shared that could not have been possible without the pooling of the financial resources of a group. (I still remember over twenty years ago when a group of Christians in San Clemente, California, purchased a bus for a neighborhood center in Watts at the time of the riots. Just recently, eight persons purchased a van for a paralyzed woman in Memphis, and twelve people have shared in paying the expense of an Estonian pastor to come to the United States for six months of theological study.)

Note your experience here and how you feel about having shared in it.

If you are a part of a church, reflect upon whether the ministry of the church would be enhanced or crippled if all persons in the church gave at the percentage level of income that you give. In light of this, pray and seek guidance about your pattern of financial giving.

Day Five: *Generosity of Life—Time*

> Now Peter and John were going up to the temple at the hour of prayer, the ninth hour. And a man lame from birth was being carried, whom they laid daily at that gate of the temple which is called Beautiful to ask alms of those who entered the temple. Seeing Peter and John about to go into the temple, he asked for alms. And Peter directed his gaze at him, with John, and said, "Look at us." And he fixed his attention upon them, expecting to receive something from them. But Peter said, "I have no silver and gold, but I give you what I have; in the name of Jesus Christ of Nazareth, walk." And he took him by the right hand and raised him up; and immediately his feet and ankles were made strong. And leaping up he stood and walked and entered the temple with them, walking and leaping and praising God.
>
> —Acts 3:1–8

There is an exciting and challenging message in this healing experience. The early Christians lived daily in expectation of miracles. They believed that what Christ had promised, he would perform. Their faith was powerful because it was so genuine, so deep and uncomplicated that it enabled them to transcend themselves and be free channels of Christ's unchecked, undiluted grace and power.

As exciting as the healing recorded in this scripture story, there is a brief word which draws our attention in another direction and offers a clear lesson about generosity. "Such as I have give I thee" (Acts 3:6, KJV). The lesson is this. God requires of each of us *such as we have.*

The gospel puts us all on common ground. The ground around the cross is level; that is, at the foot of the cross, we are all equal. But not just at the cross is the gospel a great equalizer. The requirements and the rewards come as the same to all. God requires of each of us such as we have.

Focus on *time,* our common commodity. "Such as we have": we all have it. The question is our use of it.

I doubt if there is any area of our lives in which we are more stingy. Here our selfishness shows most glaringly. We want to control our time. We schedule tightly and become irritable, even angry, when any person or happening invades that private domain.

Now, I believe in *time management.* Paul talked about redeeming time, and to the Colossians he wrote, "Conduct yourselves wisely toward outsiders, making the most of the time" (Col. 4:5). Time is so precious because it represents the total investment of our lives. Therefore, it is not to be wasted. When we waste time we are wasting ourselves. The best way to guard against wasted time is to make lists of tasks we have to perform, persons we need to see, letters to write, calls to make and to schedule those.

But there is a difference between wasting time and being generous. To be generous with our time requires at least two willing acts and/or responses.

One, in planning the use of our time we need to specifically make time for our families, loved ones, and friends. (I might add parenthetically that some of us must willingly make time for ourselves—rest, recreation, retreats for spiritual renewal.) This means that many of us, given the speed and intensity of our lives, must schedule family time, or time for fellowship with friends, and guard it.

Recently we had the joyful privilege of having all our children home for a few weeks. Kim, the oldest, was getting married. She had been away from home for five years. Kerry, the middle child, had been away at college for three years. Kevin was the only one living at home. We had some wonderful times reflecting on their childhood. Without exception, what each of them talked about most was our family time: the vacation trips, the ritual holidays of Thanksgiving and between Christmas and New Year which we spent with another family annually for ten years, the Friday-night-Saturday weekly beach days in our camper. Their sharing underscored again how important it is to make and guard time for family and friends.

Two, willingly give time not scheduled to those persons who come into your life unexpectedly. Now this is the point at which generosity of time becomes an act of love and submission which is a discipline for spiritual growth. Just yesterday, a call came to the church for a minister. I was the only minister there, and it was obvious that some stranger traveling through our city was in need of help. I almost didn't accept the call; I was so busy. Even after accepting it, I found myself defensive and unresponsive. Fortunately I caught myself, asked the Lord's forgiveness, and prayed for attentiveness and sensitivity.

The outcome of it all was that I was confronted with the need to alter a very busy day, drive downtown to the bus station and deliver some food money to this person. In my sharing with the man, Mr. Haller, I soon learned that he was "moving into" (those were his words) the Christian life from another religion, and it was a great confirmation for him that Christians would respond to his need. In the evening, following my interruption by Mr. Haller, I was working on this book, and found a word by Dietrich Bonhoeffer which added more perspective to what had happened:

> The second service that one should perform for another in a Christian community is that of active helpfulness. This means, initially, simple assistance in trifling, external matters. There is a multitude of these things wherever people live together. Nobody is

too good for the meanest service. One who worries about the loss of time that such petty, outward acts of helpfulness entail is usually taking the importance of his own career too solemnly (Bonhoeffer, p. 188).

Now it doesn't always happen that way. In most cases we never know what time given to others means in their lives. We do know, however, that scripture calls us to practice hospitality to strangers. But more than that, we know that selfishness has a strong hold on our lives, that we hoard our time for our own wishes and pleasure, and that when we give time to others we are practicing a discipline that will strike a telling blow to our self-centered, self-serving styles, and will be another step toward the cross style to which Jesus calls us.

Reflecting and Recording

Begin with the negative. During the past three weeks what calls to be generous with your time have you denied? List two or three. (If you have not denied any such calls, don't be arrogant like the Pharisee and thank God that you are "not as other men," but do thank God that you have been delivered from temptation.)

_____

_____

_____

Reflect on the reasons you refused these calls and whether you were *responsible* or simply selfish.

Now look at the way you make time for your family, loved ones, and friends. Do you need to alter your life in this respect? In the left column, list the "times" you are giving them now. If this is not generous enough, in the right column make a list of times you will start giving. Be specific by recording dates and naming what you will do with these persons.

_____   _____

_____   _____

_____   _____

_____   _____

_____   _____

If you need to contact persons to reserve some time to be with them, decide now when and how you will do that today.

Pray for the will to respond in the spirit of Christ today to whatever calls are made on your time.

Day Six: *Generosity of Life—Attention*

> Those who are unhappy have no need for anything in this world but people capable of giving them their attention. The capacity to give one's attention to a sufferer is a very rare and difficult thing; it is almost a miracle; *it is a miracle*. Nearly all those who think they have this capacity do not possess it. Warmth of heart, impulsiveness, pity are not enough. . . .
>   The love of our neighbor in all its fullness simply means being able to say to them: "What are you going through?" (Weil, p. 75)

This word of Simone Weil, the French practical mystic, sounds a challenging call to generosity of life. The call is to give our attention to others. This follows naturally our consideration of *time* yesterday. Time and attention go together. But the truth is we can give people our time without giving them our attention.

We are laying bold the claim that each one of us is called to be Christ, to be so conformed to him that we will reflect his presence in the world.

In the first chapter of his Gospel, Mark, with almost breathtaking succinctness and rapidity, tells the story of Jesus' forty days in the wilderness, his call and baptism, then his call of the disciples, and his beginning ministry. He records a series of healings. One of those healings was of a leper.

> And a leper came to him beseeching him, and kneeling said to him, "If you will, you can make me clean." Moved with pity, he stretched out his hand and touched him, and said to him, "I will; be clean." And immediately the leprosy left him, and he was made clean. And he sternly charged him, and sent him away at once, and said to him, "See that you say nothing to any one; but go, show yourself to the priest, and offer for your cleansing what

Moses commanded, for a proof to the people.'' But he went out
and began to talk freely about it, and to spread the news, so that
Jesus could no longer openly enter a town, but was out in the
country; and people came to him from every quarter.

—Mark 1:40–45

In New Testament times leprosy was the most dreaded of all
diseases. The victim not only suffered physical debilitation, but more,
mental and emotional pain and anguish. Lepers were forced to live
alone; they had to wear special clothing so others could identify them
and avoid them. Perhaps the most abysmal humiliation was that they
were required by law to announce their despicable condition: *Unclean!*

Mark tells of one of these lepers coming boldly to Jesus, kneeling
before him, and appealing, ''If you want to, you can make me clean''
(AP). Then, there is packed into one beautiful sentence almost everything Jesus *was* and *was about*. ''Jesus was filled with pity for him,
and stretched out his hand and placed it on the leper, saying, 'Of
course I want to—*be clean!*' ''(Mark 1:41, Phillips) That tells it all.
Let's stay with that encounter for a moment to get the full impact of it.
By law the leper had no right to even draw near Jesus, much less
speak to him. *How* we do not know, but the leper knew that despite his
repulsive disease, his grotesque appearance, Jesus would see him,
really *see him,* and respond to him as a person, not as a maimed,
disfigured piece of flesh. Note Jesus' response: He listened, he looked
at him, and he touched him—the three action responses that no one
else would dare make to a leper.

Let's look at these responses as our way of being generous with
our attention along with our time.

Jesus listened to the leper. Is there anything that enhances our
feelings of worth more than being listened to? When you listen to me
you say to me, ''I value you. You are important. I will hear what you
say.''

Jesus looked at him. He gave the leper his attention. When we
listen and look at another, we are attending. Someone has defined
thought as ''man in his wholeness wholly attending.'' That is more
than thought, it is an affirming relationship: a person in his or her
wholeness wholly attending another person.

Simone Weil continued the word with which we began today with
some clear teaching about how we look at another.

It is indispensable to know how to look at him in a certain way.
This way of looking is first of all attentive. The soul empties itself
of all its own contents in order to receive into itself the person it is
looking at, just as he is, in all his truth. Only he who is capable of
attention can do this (Weil, p. 75).

Jesus not only listened and looked, he touched the leper. To be generous with our attention, we cannot remain aloof; we must deliberately reach out, touch, and become involved. We will consider this aspect of attention more tomorrow.

When I give attention by looking, listening, and touching, the Spirit comes alive in relationship. When I listen and look with mind and heart, revelation comes; the gap between the other person and me is bridged. A sensitivity comes that is not my own. I feel the pain, frustration, and anguish of the other. Beyond myself and my own resources I become an instrument of miracle-working love. Healing, comfort, reconciliation, strength, and guidance come to others when we generously give them our attention by looking, listening, and touching.

Reflecting and Recording

Make the decision now that you are going to practice listening and looking in all your relationships. Begin in your most intimate settings—your family, your closest friends. But don't stop there. To be truly generous with your attention, it must be given to all whose lives intersect yours. Pray for insight and the will to follow through.

Return for a moment to Simone Weil's word at the beginning of today's discussion. She says that "warmth of heart, impulsiveness, pity are not enough" to make our generosity of attention count the most. We need to know how to look and listen. "The soul empties itself of all its own contents in order to receive into itself the person it is looking at, just as he is, in all truth." This means we must give our attention *prayerfully*. We listen for the other's sake not our own. So we must be humble and unselfish. Take this prayer with you to your listening and looking.

Lord Jesus, free me of feeling my own needs and desires in this relationship. Make me so open, accepting, and vulnerable, that _____ will be free to share her/himself with me. Deliver me from being threatened, defensive, or judgmental. I want to love as you loved. I commit my attention to you and to _____. Amen.

Day Seven: *Generosity of Life—Affirmation*

Dr. James Lynch of Johns Hopkins University has written a challenging book entitled *The Broken Heart.* In it he expresses his absolute conviction that *loneliness is the number one physical killer in America today.*

Using actuarial tables from ten years of research, Dr. Lynch tells us that individuals who live alone—single, widowed, divorced—have premature death rates from two to ten times higher than those of persons who live with others. Living alone, he says, does not necessarily produce loneliness, but the two often are related. Here are some of Dr. Lynch's revealing comparisons:

- Twice as many white divorced males under age seventy die from heart disease, lung cancer, and stomach cancer.

- Three times as many men in this category die of hypertension; seven times as many from cirrhosis of the liver.

- Among divorced people, suicide is five times higher and fatal car accidents four times higher.

- People who live alone visit physicians more frequently and stay in hospitals twice as long for identical illnesses.

What does all this mean? Dr. Lynch convincingly argues that loneliness produces physical illness and that a person literally can die of a broken heart.

Yesterday we saw how Jesus related to the leper. He listened, he looked, and he touched. Touching calls for involvement. We can't practice generosity of life by keeping persons "at arm's length" from us. Dr. Lynch's data speaks to the total question. Not just people living alone, but people from all walks of life need the caring, healing touch of Christ. That touch must come through you and me.

It centers in affirmation. People need to be affirmed, to know that they are important, that we value them, that they count in our and God's scheme of things.

Here generosity is an important discipline because again it ministers to others but also frees us from enslavement to self and our own selfish agenda. There are many ways to affirm others. Let's focus on two.

One is expressly giving the benefit of the doubt to persons with whom we are related. F. Scott Fitzgerald opened his novel, *The Great Gatsby,* with these words:

In my younger and more vulnerable years my father gave me some advice that I've been turning over in my mind ever since. "Whenever you feel like criticizing anyone," he told me, "just remember that all the people in this world haven't had the advantages that you've had."

That's good advice. In the next paragraph Fitzgerald adds to it: *"Reserving judgments is a matter of infinite hope."*

That is a powerful thought, packed with a lot of meaning. We can practice generosity by reserving judgment, by expressly giving others the benefit of the doubt, by trusting them, and expecting the very best from them.

When we judge others we are not generous. In fact, judging limits the persons we judge, puts them in a box. Not to judge is an expression of hope and expectation and is always an affirming experience for those to whom we relate.

The second way of affirmation is more selective and focused. It is a discipline of submission or service to those who obviously need it most.

When we considered the discipline of submission and service, one of the theme texts was, "Do nothing from selfishness or conceit, but in humility count others better than yourselves" (Phil. 2:3). Humility has to be practiced. William Law contended that we learn humility by learning to serve others. To become humble,

> condescend to all the weaknesses and infirmities of your fellow-creatures, cover their frailties, love their excellencies, encourage their virtues, relieve their wants, rejoice in their prosperities, compassionate their distress, receive their friendship, overlook their unkindness, forgiven their malice, be a servant of servants, and condescend to do the lowest offices to the lowest of mankind (Law, p. 26).

Law would have us serve everyone, and so it should be. But as a discipline of affirmation through serving, I'm calling for the selection of persons who desperately need affirmation. I'm thinking of

. . . . a person who has been out of work for six months and no job is in sight.

. . . . a thirty-three year old woman whose husband just left her, telling her that he doesn't love nor has he ever loved her.

. . . . a mother on welfare who is threatened by eviction because she is two months behind in her rent.

. . . . a preacher who has just moved and his new appointment is apparently a demotion professionally.

. . . . an obese man who has just failed to get the dream job of his life with a church agency and is certain that his weight kept him from getting the job.

These persons come to my mind as I write. They are all persons who because of their particular situation need special affirmation now. How will I respond? I will continue to counsel with the thirty-three-year old woman. I will give an anonymous check through a neighborhood center for the mother on welfare. I will be especially attentive in the months ahead to the preacher who feels "demoted" professionally. I'm not sure about the obese fellow. I simply don't know what to do. I will pray for him and stay open to some leading as to some particular way to affirm him.

Reflecting and Recording

Ponder the statement, "Reserving judgments is a matter of infinite hope." What changes does that call for in your style of relating?

Make a commitment that you will daily practice the discipline of generosity, affirming others by giving them the benefit of the doubt, trusting them and expecting the very best from them.

Make a list of at least four or five persons you know who need affirmation. Put their names in the blanks.

_____

_____

_____

_____

_____

Now beside each name, make some notes of specific ways you might affirm these people by giving them your attention.

This is the last day to specifically consider the discipline of generosity. Think for a while as to how you are going to practice this discipline in an ongoing way. The more specific your plans, the more effective will be your discipline.

Group Meeting for Week Six

Introduction

This is the last meeting designed for this group. It may be that you will want to continue meeting for a few more weeks. If so, you will need to decide that, plan your meetings, and decide whether you will use any sort of study resource such as we noted in Week Four. You may consider selecting two or three of the weeks in this workbook and going through them again as an extension of your time together. Let the group decide.

Sharing Together

Note to Leader: Save at least ten minutes for 4 and 5 in these suggestions for sharing.

1. Again follow the pattern of letting each person share his or her most meaningful and most difficult days.

2. It is not easy to talk about money, but we need to do so. Are there persons in the group who have been tithing for six months or more? Let them tell their story, how they came to this commitment and what it means to them.

3. On Day One, in the inventory of your "all" and the parable of giving up all, what would you find among the things listed as well as what you added, most difficult to give up? Let persons in the group share and discuss what the group seems to be saying about what we value most.

4. Discuss the meaning of the generosity of time, attention, and affirmation. Let the bottom line be, If I took these disciplines seriously, what changes would be required of me?

5. Give an opportunity for persons to talk about the most significant insights that have come during the six weeks—the feelings, the reservations, the doubts, the joys.

Praying Together

1. Begin your time of prayer by asking each person to express gratitude to God in a two- or three-sentence prayer for something significant that has happened to him/her as a result of these six weeks.

2. Since this may be the last meeting, some persons in the group may have special concerns or personal needs for which they wish the group to pray. Share those and offer sentence prayers in response.

3. Give each person the opportunity to share whatever decision or commitment he or she has made, or will make, to an ongoing life of discipline. Be specific. Follow each person's verbalizing of these decisions and commitment by some other person in the group praying a brief prayer of thanksgiving and support for this person.

4. A benediction is a blessing or greeting shared with another or by a group in parting. The ''passing of the peace'' is such a benediction. You take a person's hands, look into his or her eyes and say, ''The peace of God be with you,'' and the person responds, ''And may God's peace be yours.'' Then that person, taking the hands of the person next to him or her, says ''The peace of God be with you,'' and receives the response, ''And may God's peace be yours.'' Standing in a circle, let the leader ''pass the peace,'' and let it go around the circle.

5. Having completed the passing of the peace, speak to one another in a more spontaneous way. Move about to different persons in the group, saying whatever you feel is appropriate for your parting blessing to each person. Or, you may simply embrace the person and say nothing. In your own unique way, ''bless'' each person who has shared this journey with you.

References

Sources quoted in this workbook are identified in the text by author and page number. If more than one work by the same author is cited, the title of the work is included in the citation. Bibliographic information for each source is listed below.

Amiel, Henri-Frederic. *Amiel's Journal*. Translated by Mrs. Humphrey Ward. London: Macmillan, 1889.

Barclay, William. *The Letters to Timothy, Titus and Philemon*. Philadelphia: Westminster, 1975.

Bloom, Anthony. *Living Prayer*. London: Darton, Longman and Todd, 1966.

Bonhoeffer, Dietrich. *Life Together*. New York: Harper & Row, 1954.

Buechner, Frederick. *Wishful Thinking*. New York: Harper & Row, 1973.

Calkin, Ruth Harms. *Tell Me Again, Lord, I Forget*. Elgin, IL: David C. Cook, 1974.

The Cloud of Unknowing. Edited by James Walsh. Ramsey, NJ: Paulist Press, 1981.

Coffin, William Sloan, Jr. *Once to Every Man*. New York: Atheneum, 1977.

Day, Albert Edward. *Discipline and Discovery*. Workbook ed. adapted by Danny E. Morris. Nashville: Upper Room, 1977.

Doherty, Catherine de Hueck. *Poustinia: Christian Spirituality of the East for Western Man*. Notre Dame: Ave Maria, 1975.

Donnelly, Doris. *Learning to Forgive*. New York: Macmillan, 1979.

Dumitriu, Petru. *To the Unknown God*. New York: Seabury, 1982.

Dunnam, Maxie. *Alive in Christ*. Nashville: Abingdon, 1982.

—————. *Galatians, Ephesians, Philippians, Colossians, Philemon*. Vol. 8, *The Communicator's Commentary*. Waco, TX: Word, 1982.

Edwards, Tilden. *Living Simply Through the Day*. New York: Paulist Press, 1977.

Fénelon, Mme. Guyon et al. *A Guide to True Peace*. New York: Harper & Brothers, 1946.

Foster, Richard J. *Celebration of Discipline*. San Francisco: Harper & Row, 1978.

King, Martin Luther. *Strength to Love*. Cleveland, OH: Collins-World, 1963.

Kunkel, Fritz. *In Search of Maturity*. New York: Scribner, 1943.

Langford, Thomas A. *Christian Wholeness*. Nashville: Upper Room, 1978.

Law, William. *A Serious Call to a Devout and Holy Life*. Arranged and edited by Thomas S. Kepler. Living Selections from the Great Devotional Classics. Nashville: Upper Room, 1952.

Lawrence, Brother. *The Practice of the Presence of God*. New York: Fleming H. Revell, 1895.

Leech, Kenneth. *True Prayer*. San Francisco: Harper & Row, 1980.

Lynch, James. *The Broken Heart*. New York: Basic, 1977.

May, Rollo. *Love and Will*. New York: Norton, 1969.

Merton, Thomas. *Contemplation in a World of Action*. New York: Doubleday, 1971.

—————. *The Sign of Jonas*. New York: Harcourt, Brace, Jovanovich, 1953.

Nouwen, Henri J. M. *Clowning in Rome*. Garden City: Image, 1979.

O'Connor, Flannery. *The Habit of Being, Letters of Flannery O'Connor.* New York: Farrar, Straus & Giroux, 1979.

Ortiz, Juan Carlos. *The Disciple.* Wheaton, IL: Creation House, 1975.

Phillips, John Bertram. *When God Was Man.* Nashville: Abingdon, 1955.

Ruskin, John. *Modern Painters.* Vol. 3. New York: Lovell, Coryell and Company, 1865.

Steere, Douglas V. *Together in Solitude.* New York: Crossroad, 1982.

Stewart, George S. *The Lower Levels of Prayer.* New York: Abingdon-Cokesbury, 1939.

Underhill, Evelyn. *Concerning the Inner Life.* London: Methuen, 1926.

Watson, Bernard. *A Hundred Years' War: The Salvation Army 1865-1965.* London: Hodder and Stoughton, 1964.

Weil, Simone. *Waiting on God.* London: Collins Fontana, 1963.

Wesley, John. *Wesley's Standard Sermons.* Vol. 1. Nashville: M.E. Church South, 1787.

Additional Reading

Barclay, William. *The Daily Study Bible.* 18 Volumes. Philadelphia: Westminster, 1975.

This series of volumes on each book in the New Testament is easy to read, insightful, and practical. There is no Bible study resource I would recommend more highly.

Day, Albert. *Discipline and Discovery.* Ashland, OH: Disciplined Order of Christ, 1977.

Along with *Celebration of Discipline* by Richard J. Foster, this is a contemporary classic on spiritual disciplines. Danny Morris has adapted Discipline and Discovery into a very helpful workbook edition published by The Upper Room.

Dunnam, Maxie. *Workbook of Living Prayer.* Nashville: Upper Room, 1974.
————. *Workbook of Intercessory Prayer.* Nashville: Upper Room, 1979.

If you have not used these two workbooks previously, you may want to continue your group with one of them as a basic resource. The format is the same as this workbook.

Foster, Richard J. *Celebration of Discipline.* San Francisco: Harper & Row, 1978.

This is the most valuable book I know in the area of spiritual discipline.

Job, Rueben P. *A Journey Toward Solitude and Community.* Nashville: Upper Room, 1982.

Following a workbook format, this excellent retreat resource is available as a participant's workbook and a separate leader's guide.

Langford, Thomas A. *Christian Wholeness.* Nashville: Upper Room, 1978.

One of numerous works on the Christian life and way. Thomas Langford's book is an excellent exploration of Christian wholeness.